T4-AHV-651

DISCARDED

*Title* ANTHROPOLOGICAL REPORT

ON THE

IBO-SPEAKING PEOPLES OF NIGERIA.

BY

NORTHCOTE W. THOMAS, M.A., F.R.A.I., ETC..

GOVERNMENT ANTHROPOLOGIST.

PART V.

# ADDENDA TO IBO-ENGLISH DICTIONARY.

NEGRO UNIVERSITIES PRESS
NEW YORK

Originally published in 1914
by Harrison and Sons, London

Reprinted 1969 by
Negro Universities Press
A DIVISION OF GREENWOOD PUBLISHING CORP.
NEW YORK

SBN 8371-1462-4

PRINTED IN UNITED STATES OF AMERICA

# PREFACE.

The present volume contains firstly the Addenda and Corrigenda of the Ibo Dictionary previously published, the proofs of which were read mainly in the colony, so that comparison with the original MS. was impossible.

In the second place it contains re-determinations of tones of certain words in the previous Dictionary, and in the third place a number of words used in the Asaba dialect. It must be understood that these latter by no means comprise the whole of the Asaba vocabulary; words included in the previous Dictionary are not reprinted here.

The tones were noted on the assumption, which has since turned out to be incorrect, that they are four in number, high, low, and upper and lower middle. Reference to Part VI will show that by the study of phonograph records many more tones have been discovered. As, however, words pronounced according to the number notation adopted in this Dictionary appear to be recognisable, even if they are not absolutely accurate, I have not hesitated to print my data here. In a certain number of cases, material collected at an early stage of my tour was left unrevised, and in such, words are, as a rule, marked with accents only.

The whole of the material was collected personally, and I have made no attempt to incorporate material collected either by the Church Missionary Society or the Roman Catholic Mission at Asaba. A request addressed to the Church Missionary Society in 1910 for permission to study their material was refused. I mentioned the subject informally at the Roman Catholic Mission, but made no definite proposal. In view of the fact that comparatively little of my time is devoted to linguistic research, it would have been impossible to revise with due care material collected by other people, and it is undesirable to include in any Dictionary data collected at different hands unless comparative uniformity is obtained by careful revision.

The main mass of the Dictionary refers to the Asaba language, but in certain cases words from the Hinterland and from the east of the Niger are included, as also certain words accidentally omitted from the Onitsha-Awka Dictionary. Such words are shown by a letter or other abbreviation in brackets. The short time available for the collection of material in the colony prevented me from examining in detail many points of interest. Thus g lenis is found in a certain number of words, and the table of consonants shows two or more variants of the same consonant are in use.

NORTHCOTE W. THOMAS.

# PHONETIC ELEMENTS.

## CONSONANTS.

b,

ḅ, with glottal stop.

č, ch as in *church*.

d,

ḍ, cerebral d.

f,

f̱, bilabial.

g,

g̱, uvular (?).

ɣ, " soft " (fricative) g as in N. German *tag*.

h,

ǰ, as in *judge*.

k,

ḳ, uvular (?)

l,

m,

n,

palatalised n is written ny

ṅ, ng as in *singer*.

p,

ṗ, with glottal stop.

r,

rh, breathed r.

s,

ṣ, cerebral s.

š, as sh.

t,

ṭ, cerebral t.

ṯ, has something of a th sound; it is formed by putting
the tongue against the upper teeth.

v,

v̩, bilabial v.

v̥, unvoiced v.

w,

y,

z,

ž, as zh.

## VOWELS.

ạ, short a, as in French *ma*.

a̠, long a.

e, close e, resembles French e in *été*.

ẹ, ę, as in *let*, *there*, very open.

ị, į, open i.

i, as in French *ici*.

ọ, ǫ, very open o.

o̠, less open, found after ḍ, r, g, etc.

o̩, slightly open.

o, French o, as in *eau*.

ọ, close o, perhaps with overrounding.

ụ, ų, very open u, sounding almost like o.

u, close u.

## DIPHTHONGS.

ai,

au, especially in dialectical forms such as dau for do.

oa,

oi,

' after a vowel signifies abrupt close.

ˎ below a vowel indicates a specially long, usually con-
tracted, vowel.

˜ sign of nasalisation.

' sign of palatalisation.

## Consonants.

b appears to be in some cases more fully voiced than in others.

ɓ sounds like a very fully voiced b : it is, however, probable that the glottal stop really exists, for such forms as ibo (more properly written iɓo) are pronounced igbo by neighbouring tribes ; and the third person of 'ɓue, to kill, is in the Ǫka dialect ogbue, the g being distinctly heard ; but the main audible difference between ɓue, kill and bue, carry, is that the former is more fully voiced. Where the preceding k is pronounced, however, the b is only partially voiced, if at all.

In the words printed in the Dictionary, kp, a considerable proportion might well be written kb.

c, j. I omitted to determine whether j and c are front plosives or affricates. From the phonetic changes from which they are due, the latter is more probable.

d, also t, are occasionally cerebral. t (ṭ) appears to be interdental in a certain number of cases, in giving a sound nearer th than the ordinary English t. d lenis appears to be found sometimes.

f, v. It is exceedingly difficult in many cases to determine whether f is denti-labial or bilabial, but the distinction does not appear to be of any importance for the meaning of the word. It is often said that v is not found, in point of fact an unvoiced v is by no means uncommon.

g appears to be voiced in different degree. It is also found as a lenis, for example in ago, leopard. A systematic distinction between the lenis and fortis is not made in the Dictionary owing to lack of time for the revision of the material in the Colony.

In addition to the ordinary g, a uvular (?) g is found, shown as g̣. This I termed postvelar g in Part III of this report. It is only very slightly explosive. The same applies to ḳ. It may be that this g̣ and ḳ are in reality fricative, for in whispered words the k sound seems to disappear altogether and to be replaced by h. On the whole, however, I am disposed to think that they are stopped, not fricative.

h is only rarely found ; but in certain areas, such as Isele Asaba, it appears as an intrusive letter between two vowels.

l in a certain number of cases, appears to be formed much the same way as in English. In other cases the tongue does not touch the palate, but makes a semicircular movement to the left, and then returns to the central position. The sound thus produced is almost indistinguishable from n and r. The distinction between this l and the other one is not made in the Dictionary.

ṅ. There is some uncertainty about words which are printed in the Dictionary under ṅk. Such words as ṅkpu might just as well be written mpu, where m bears the same relation to the ordinary m as ṅ does to n.

rh is written for a breathed r very frequent in the Asaba language. It is also found at Nimo on the other side of the Niger, and in the Edo languages (see Report on the Edo-Speaking Peoples).

š is interchangeable with r (rh).

b, m and other consonants are sometimes followed by a diphthong, of which one component is usually o, this is printed bw, mw, etc., where the word is not found with a simple m or b it should be looked for under bw, mw, etc.

In a certain number of words the division into syllables is unusual ; such are abamwọ (ab-amwọ) akwu (ak-wu), anagala (anag-ala), ọ̃gogo (ọg-ogo), ọ̃kò (ọk-o), ičoku (ičok-u), ígwè (ig-we), obẹle (ob-ẹle), ọ́kò (ọk-o) ; there is perhaps a simultaneous glottal stop. But this explanation will hardly meet the cases nwagẹlẹle (nwagẹl-ẹle), onyinyo (onyin-yo), úmẹ̃ (um-e), ẹbẹnẹbe (ẹbẹn-ẹbe), ala (al-a), alolo (al-olo) amabwa (am-abwa).

## VOWELS.

The Asaba vowel sounds appear to be more complicated than those of Ọka. This is possibly due to better opportunities for observation.

a, which is found both long and short, is a very forward sound, especially in such words as ča, ja, where the consonant may be a front plosive.

ǫ is extremely open; ǫ appears to be slightly diphthongated with a preceding closed o.

o̱ is found after d, r, l, and g. Do̱ is pronounced as though the d were cerebral, but its association with other consonants shows that the vowel itself has the distinctive value. It is a tense vowel pronounced with the tip of the tongue raised.

ǫ is open, but less so than the preceding; o is a very common sound and appears to be the same as French o in eau. This frequently is the first component of a diphthong, especially after m, b, f before a.

ọ is a very close o found in only a few cases, especially after w. It resembles the North German o in boot.

u̱ is a very o-like sound and is usually heard and written as o until attention is directed to it.

i̱, three varieties of open i are found, as in li̱, pï̱, či̱, with diminishing degrees of openness; but as it is unnecessary to distinguish between them in order to differentiate words of different meaning they are all indicated with one symbol. The very open i in li̱ might almost be described as a very narrow e, resembling a French e.

All Ibo verbs prefix a or e to the root consonant to form the present tense and also with the verbal form used with the Negative, Continuative, and Future Auxiliaries. a is used with all verbs of which the root vowel is a or an open vowel; e with all verbs of which the root vowel is e or a close vowel. This law enables us to say that the open u and open i mentioned above are in really u and i and not close o and e.

Any monosyllabic verb without indication of vowel length has not been revised, and is of uncertain vowel quality.

With regard to the system of transliteration it should be noted that except in monosyllables the final e is usually if not invariably open. The formative vowel noted in Part III has been omitted in the present Dictionary in view of the fact that the use of a or e depends upon a very simple law; a is used where the first vowel of the verb is a or an open vowel, e where it is e or a closed vowel. Owing to this difference of the formative vowel we find that the pronoun in the third person singular of the a verbs is ǫ, of the o verbs is o, and the initial vowel of the infinitive of the a verbs appears to be open, while that of the e verbs is closed.

The data at my disposal make it somewhat uncertain whether the final e of monosyllabic verbs follows the rule mentioned above. Thus the vowel of the 3rd person singular appears to be o, and the root vowel of the verb makes on the ear the impression of closeness ; in the phonograph record, on the other hand, the vowel is distinctly open.

Final e in other words appears to vary in sound ; it is sometimes distinctly open, but sometimes seems to stand midway between open and closed. No systematisation has been attempted with such words.

# TONES.

The Dictionary was prepared in the colony on the assumption that four tones should be distinguished; this assumption is shown by the phonograph records to be incorrect (see Part VI).

The high tone is shown by ′ or by a small 1 above the vowel; the low tone by ‵ or a small 4; the middle tone by ‾ or, in the case of the words collected towards the end of the tour, by a small 2 (upper middle) or 3 (lower middle).

In monosyllabic words especially the high tone is usually short; ′ at the end of the word marks a short vowel with abrupt close; where the tone is not given it may be assumed to be high. Where numbers in brackets follow a word they indicate the tones upon the successive syllables.

Compound tones, usually rising, are indicated by the two components thus : dö̈.

# TABLE OF CONTENTS.

# ABBREVIATIONS.

In abbreviation, H = Hinterland.
Al. = Ala.
As. = Asaba.
At. = Atoma.
A, O = Awka, Oniča.
I A = Isele Asaba.
Ib. = Ibuzǫ.
Idum = Idumuje.
O = Oniča.
Ob. = Oboluku.
Obo = Obǫmpa.
Og. = Ogwashi.
Okp. = Okpanam.
O. O. = Oniča Olona.
Ubul = Ubulubu.
Uk. = Ukunzu.
a = aorist.
p = present.

# IBO-ENGLISH DICTIONARY.

# IBO-ENGLISH DICTIONARY.

Àba, Aba (town).

àbǎ, gaping wound.

àbà', staple (used in making medicine).

àbà', flat.

ababǎla, wide and flat.

abača, cassava (A).

abǎdî, sea (O).

abaǰala, wide and flat.

àbàm, edge, corner, and roof.

abananĕ, yam species.

abanęke, yam species.

abani (Edo : ębę), ceremonial sword.

àbǎzǔ (mili, osisi, úbwǒ), broad, spreading.

àbî, a white yam.

abįbia, helpless.

abibiači, stupid.

abialu, stupid.

àbǒ̈, pus (O).

àbǒ (ų̇zǫ̇), cross roads ; abo nabǫ, fork in road.

ằbǒ, armpit (O).

àbǫ̇, basket (long).

ǒnyé àbǫ̇', companion.

àbǫ̇ (ókwằ), plantation.

aboa n'abǫ, two by two.

ầbǒbǒ, bead (kind).

ầbǒbo, mashed yam, palm husk.

abǒbwa idide, worm castings.

abǫši, back door.

abų (the finder says : abum), "find."

ăbụ́, song (O).

abuba akainya, leaf fronds (bambu).

àbůbá', fat.

àbụ̆bwȧ nti, cheek in front of ear.

àbụ̆bwọ̣ (ogẹde), husk of banana, etc., bark; skin (yam, fish).

abuke (I.A.), dish for ikenga.

abule, careless.

àbúlú akwụ, mashed palm nuts.

àbuọ̣', Abo (town).

abụzụ, cricket.

abwa (Okp.), poverty.

àbwá' (A), jawbone, lower (?)

abwá', arrangement.

àbwȧ, rendezvous; appointed day.

abwa ofili, planks with mud on top (in house against fire).

àbwȧdȧ, knife, two-edged.

ᾰbwȧlȧ, four-cornered seat.

ᾰbwȧlȧ, rich women (not old) who have borne two or three children.

àbwᾰlȧ, hairy seed.

abwalagada, tall.

abwamimi (Okp.), kind of basket

ábwanare, two people of same height; sort of matchet in sheath.

abwano, stupid.

abwanučе, marks under eyes.

abwẹ, calabash, float.

abwẹle, semicircular marks (under breast).

abwẹle, stomach marks.

abwẹli, division of irhe.

abwigwe, blue sky (day); open sky.

Aḃwọ̣, Agbor (town).

àbwọ̣, cloth (cover).

àbwọ̣: seed, stock, generation, Okafọ̣ bụ ẹzibo àbwọ̣, O is of a good stock.

àbwȯ, puerperal fever (?)

åbwọ̀, calabash of water.

åbwò', climbing rope made of palm fibre (ekwẹle); rope for tying prisoner.

åbwồ, thick cord (from chewed palm nuts).

åbwồ, palaver.

åbwồ, tangle.

åbwồ, (ewu, okp̀oro), prolific (goat, woman).

abwogala, large (living creature).

abwokili, armlet.

abwolo, weak (sun).

abwŏlo, echo.

abwologada, back teeth, strong man.

abwonọ, straight (hair), soft.

abwọno, mango.

ačanu, blue bead, hindrance.

ačẹle, yam species.

åčîčá, dried yam haulm.

åčîčå, biscuit; dried yam.

åčŏ (H), pine apple.

ặdå', fall.

ådá akwa, first sickness of child.

adadalani, floor.

ådằ, daughter, eldest.

ådằ, adẹbo, head woman of ẹbo, etc.

ắdằkằ, lump on back of hand.

ådằkằ, monkey.

ådằkằ, yam.

ådằkằ, gun, short and thick.

adani, room in boy's house.

ada okwo, stay-at-home, one who does not visit others.

adaru, torrent, flowing down.

ådằrᷜ, upside down.

ada ụnọ, oldest woman of umunna.

adei, long time.

ådềî (ni), long ago.

ådềî li, long ago.

adẹle, mate, companion.

ạdo, " yam that bears seeds."

ádú, ill treatment caused by envy.

ạ̀dụ̈, bitter kola.

ạ̀fạ̊ (A), divination.

ã̀fạ̊, name.

afa ẹgu, dance name.

afa olili, work name.

afa ọlụ, work name.

afẹke (=agẹne), mat.

afẹle akwã̱ ọkoko, (like an egg) china plate.

ạ̀fiạ̊, keeping secret.

ạ̀fiạ̊, heddle (loom).

afia nabi (O. O), cloth with two stripes.

ạ̀fĩfiạ̊, boil in throat.

ạ̀fọ́, belly.

ạ̀fọ̣̀, fish.

ạ̀fọ̣̀, afo day (fourth day of the week).

ã̱fọ̊fọ̊, " measles."

ã̱fọ̊fọ̊, rain water.

afọ ạgwa', fish species.

ạ̀fọ̣̀ (Og.), disease.

ạ̀fọ́ḿbwali, áfọ́ḿbwàfi, turning stomach.

afọ nta, side (of abdomen).

afọ nupu, loose bowels (after laxative or naturally).

afọ ọgiga, loose bowels.

afọ okṗi, big stomach.

afọ ụkṗa, big stomach.

ạ̀fũ̈fá, tomato.

ã̱fụ́fụ́, labour, trouble.

afufu (Abọ), breeze.

áfụ̈lụ̈, " So sorry, I haven't got it " (in proverbs).

ạ̀fụ̈lụ̈, empty.

ạ̀fụ̈lụ̈, bullet.

ạ̀fụ̈ lụ́ ụzụ, slag.

agạ̊', a white yam.

ạ̀gã̱', adze.

ạ̀gạ̊ (A), sterile woman.

ạgạ̀dạ̀, chair, folding ; wooden sword.

agadằga, a red yam.

agadằga, yam (abana).

agalama, not new ; ripe kola, properly dry.

agalŏwa, reed sp.

ạgạ̀ma (O), clitoris.

agama, fish spear (one point).

agฮalagada (O), thunder.

agbwe (Abwọ), hoe.

agẹliga (A), kind of spear.

agidi, paste of corn.

agili (O), bullet.

agini, mat.

ágạ́ (Onička Olona), cup.

ạgỏ̀, kite.

ạgỏ̀, farm.

ạgỏ̃ (a)gu [ago'(n)agu], be hungry.

ằgỏ̀', leopard.

ạgỏ̀, hunger.

ago iฅiฅi, fly sp. (striped).

ạgỡ̋lỏ̀, thin (liquid).

ạgỏ̀lỏ̀, bird lime.

ằgolo, fish species.

ạgu, mesh (small).

ạgủ, garden.

ạgủgwạ̀, bush rope.

aguma, clever.

agụnta, bellyache (child).

agwa, pied (animal).

agwaka, snake sp.

agwằla, giant.

ạgwé (Al.), hoe.

ạinyạ̀', cane (big, thick), bush rope.

ạinyạ̀, eye.

ainya akฮoru(m), (I) am weak.

ainya ẹฮbwẹ̀, squint.

ainya mili, line from inner angle of eye to ear.

ainya mpi, one-eyed.

åinyå', lying in bush to seize people.

ainya ṅwolo, space between rows of yams in fence.

ainya naliṅali (A), hazel eyes.

ainya ṅgẹlẹgọ, squint.

ainya ṅkpọlọ, one-eyed.

ainyanni, handful of fufu.

ainyanti, careless person, who does not listen.

ainya ọičča, "empty eye": disappointments.

ainya úfiẻ, red eyes.

åinyå uɣiẻ, squint.

ainyuku, mesh (big).

ainyaṅwu 'toto, morning star.

åinyịkẻ, axe.

ainyo (= ainyịke), axe.

åiyå, plates, etc.

aỉyå', war.

(onye) aiyanne ṅwanne (O. O), red yam.

aiyelẽya, wastrel.

aiyẹ̃liya, girl who refuses to marry.

aiyiwe (As.), salutation for Ezubwo.

áiyỉyọ̀ (also aḷiliọ), begging.

áiyỉyọ̀, cunning.

aiyo, stick of skin of manatee, used by obi.

aỉyọ̀, loosely spun cotton for warp.

ãiyobwe, fly whisk (cord).

aiyŏlo, bee-eater.

áǰå, tree; musical instruments (from pod).

åǰå, earth, dust, sand.

åǰå, fish species.

åǰå', sacrifice; áfůlům åǰå, I see a sacrifice.

aǰa ṅgwẹle, innumerable things.

aǰa, odido, mud building.

aǰa olọ, clay.

åǰårů, ill luck, sickness.

aǰẹǰiọta, hornet sp., yellow.

åǰi', (O), hair, fur, body-hair (human).

ăjî, tree species.

ajĭ bwăjĭ, big man.

åjiî, (A) crocodile, (cataphractus).

ajĭku, eyebrow.

ájŏ, disease, headache, giddiness, vomiting, and then pain in centre of sternum.

ajǫ afǫ, vexation.

åjǚ (jioko), crown (of plantains).

åjǚ, head pad.

ajɥani, ? puff adder (short and thick ; blunt tail).

ăjǚjǚ, question, demand.

åkă, old.

åkå, share in doing:—aka adǫrǫm, I had no ——.

åkå', hand, side, bank.

åkå, insect, lives in wood, bites—

áká tál'akàm, an insect bites my hand.

aká nafùm ófú n'aká, an insect hurts my hand.

åkå, date, counting (O).

aka (Uk.) brown snake.

åkåbŏ, (O.) stool.

akaduči, circular mark on cheek.

akafu, last year.

åkåinyå ènyî, eyelash of elephant.

akakala (Ib.) akikala, (Al.) crab.

åkåkƀǫ, short.

ákăkƀolo, (O), old (thing), last year's dry corn.

ăkålå, line, straight.

åkålá, (O), cake (yam, corn, etc.).

ǫnwǫm åkålǫkå, I have a cake.

åkålà, staves for ikum.

akalanti, mark at outer margin of eye.

akaliru, (A), wrinkles, lines.

ǫnwǫm ăkålĭrů, I have wrinkles.

ákalŏgŏli, slave.

ăkåmbǫ, pangolin (?)

åkånăkå, jug.

ákånčĭčă, patches of leucoderma.

åkåṅgwẹ̀, pepper pounder.

åkánĩ, yonder.

åkạ̃nĩ, (O). foolish anger.

aká ṅkp̃ilikp̃i, lost arm, lost finger.

åkáṅkwå, withered hand.

akaṅpume (As), handle of stone.

akantagide, niggardly.

akanzọ, whitlow.

akausọni, withered hand.

akaši, pole (two-pointed) for net.

akatăka, fearless man.

akatakp̃u, huge.

akatọ, mesh (medium).

åkᵬå, stout.

ắkᵬå, corner iron.

åkᵬå, fruit (lime, mango, orange, odala).

åkᵬå, speechless.

åkᵬå, insects' nest.

akᵬa, game played with pieces of calabash.

akᵬa, five shillings.

akᵬa abŭdu, salt bag.

akᵬa ẹ̃jike (abudu), salt bag (also for kernels).

akᵬå nwa mili, bladder.

åkᵬågo, trap (leopard, &c.).

åkᵬáka, ọ kbaka (akbaka), oil bean.

åkᵬăkå (Onitsha: ắkᵬåkå), creeper (seed, eaten).

akᵬāká (A), bag.

ákå, bead—

    áka nafum òfù n'aká, a bead hurts my hand.

akᵬákà (aṅwu) (O), honeycomb, wax.

akᵬākàla (A), wallet (for traveller).

akᵬakolo, open calabash.

akᵬakᵬa, small tortoise.

akᵬalaji (O), yam, moderate sized.

akᵬalakᵬa (O), long.

akᵬalaṅkụ (A), palm tree (very big).

åkᵬålåtå, frame for yams.

akɓampulu, bag with hole.

akɓamwạnu, yellow, dark fawn (as ene).

akɓani, shield (palm mid rib).

ảkɓảnkả, stubborn.

akɓankwo, beetle.

akɓa olŏko, bag for fish, etc. (round).

ảkɓảtả, drying place, bed for corn, platform.

akɓata obwadu, granary (in field).

akɓátàkɓa (O), big.

akbatẹnu, akbatani, floor of ikum tower.

ảkɓẹ́lẹ̀ (? 4-2-2), long calabash flute.

akɓa ukẹle, thick set (tall or short).

akɓa uluke, thick set (tall or short).

ảkɓílî, throat.

akɓilikɓa, fish scale.

akɓịlị̇ nta, larynx.

ảkɓọ̀, day-blindness.

ákɓọ̀ (A), knot.

ảkɓọ́ (O), yams (red) grated.

akɓo agwẹgwe, ground cassava.

akɓọii, fish sp.

akɓoji (O), small yam, seed yam left in ground.

akɓoji akɓoji (ṅwa) (O), well grown boy.

akɓokalakṗo, big swellings, rough (skin), knotty (tree).

akɓokili kɓokili (ṅwa) (O), well grown boy.

akbụ̣ḳwụ, malleolus.

akɓola, tympanites.

akɓoli, wave.

ảkɓŏlŏ ẹkwe, stem of tie-tie.

ảkɓŏlŏ, tree sp.

ảkɓŏlŏ, bag of salt.

akbolo, atresia vaginae.

akɓolo (Okp.), poverty.

akɓologadakɓo, lump (on tree).

ạkɓolu (A), spleen, inflammation of.

akboluku, overseers of work.

akɓọmạna, yellow.

akḅọmwạna (A), fawn (colour).

åkbȯṅkwo, place where palm branches part from stem.

ẵkḅȯtụ̃kbȯ̇ (A), proud flesh in marks; rough skin (small roughnesses).

ákḅụ̇ (—nkọno, O), cassava.

ẵkḅů, tumour, swelling.

   ẹ̇ṅwẹ̇lům åkbů, I have a tumour, swelling.

ẵkḅụ, cotton tree.

åkḅụ́, chin.

åkḅụ̇, seed.

åkbů àbụ (O), boil in armpit.

   éṅwệlům åkḅů åbụ̇, I have a boil in my armpit.

akḅụ aka (O), person with big forearms, biceps.

akḅụ akbị̣li, Adam's apple (O).

ákḅụ arụ̣, buttock.

akḅụ ẹlili, knot.

akḅụ mili, varicose veins of calf.

akbụ n'udẹne, Adam's apple.

akḅụ onu, goitre.

akḅụ osisi, lump, excrescence on tree.

akḅukḅọ ụ̣kwụ, boot.

akḅụlụkḅu (O), swelled cheek.

akḅuluke, short.

akḅwakulu, stomach.

akḅwibo (O.), woman's market bag.

ạ́kḅwŏnù, goitre.

ạke, hunchback.

akẹdi, dwarf.

akẽ̈ge, green snake.

åkệká, ant (makes heap [nkpu]).

åkệká, mark on house.

akẹ̈kḅe (A), left hand.

ẵkệlė̇, action.

åkẽ̈le, thin.

akẹle (ku, kpo), drum (wood).

akẹti, tree; fibres used for cloth.

akikala (Al.), crab.

ăkįkǫ́ (O), story.

ákįkǫ̀, ăkę̀lę̀kǫ̀, mussel shell.

åkĭtĭ, short.

akiti, half-grown!palm tree.

ăkǫ̀, palm nut, (after husk is removed).

ặkŏ, edible clay (black or white) ; ? lignite.

åkŏ, ant, black, winged.

åkǫ̀, chalk (lump).

åkŏ, pubic hair.

åkǫ́, arrow.

akǫ nko, barb (arrow) (spear).

akǫ'ṅkpofųlų, unfeathered arrow.

åkǫ̰ étĭleti (O), palm kernel.

ặkǫ̰ nkp̓ú, flying ant.

åkǫ̀', riches.

ák̰ŏani, plant sp.

akoba (Ezi), rat trap.

åkŏibo, koko nut.

akǫiča, vain, useless.

akoǰi, deep.

akoǰi, corner, interior.

åkŏkŏ, refuser, refusal.

akoko kala, side mark (chest).

akǫ liakǫ, bad walker.

akolo, large night jar (?)

åkŏ̃lŏ (O), sense (lit., kidneys).

åkŏlŏ (O), dog tic.

åkŏlŏ (O), things for dress (cloth, beads, etc.).

ặkŏlŏ, fungus (on rotten palm).

ặkŏlŏ (O), " back slang "—
   åsŏlûm åkŏlŏ wę̀kŭ, I speak back slang.

akotu (O.O.), big roots.

àkp̓à (O), dumb.

akp̓ačalainya (A), on purpose.

akp̓ăǰuǰu (O), fear (small).

akp̓ăla (otiti), thunder—
   akp̓ăla tie, it is thundering.

akpala dibia, bird sp. (water).

akpalaǰiǰi (A), fear (small).

akpắm, quarrel that will cause injury to originator.

åkpåtằ, "music."

akpata (Abọ́), prawn (big).

akpata oyi, goose flesh.

åkpẹ̀lị̀kpằ, scales.

akpị̀li udẹne, Adam's apple.

akpị̀li uku, gullet.

akpọ, ophthalmia.

(ndi) akpoluku, leaders of workers (one obwo).

åkpûlû ẹkwe, unsplit cane, tie-tie.

akpwakpwa, top (toy).

åkü', (O), shutter (window), door.

åkụ̀, property.

åkụ̀kụ̀, vexation, bitterness.

ẵkùkwằ, pains after child bearing, caused by clot (?)

ẵkukwanne, children by one mother.

åkụ̀m, hippopotamus.

åkûm, convulsions.

åkụ̀nsu, seedling palm.

akunti, tumour near ear.

ẵkwá, lamentation.

åkwẵ', egg—
    nyẹm åkwẵ' iṅwẹ̀lû (O), give me the egg that you have.

ẵkwằ, 1,200 cowries.

ẵkwằ (O), cloth.

(onye) akwẹte, freeborn man.

akwụ (As.), widow's house.

akwu, fence for fish (ikum).

åḳwụ̀', farm (deserted).

ẵḳwù, palm nut (before husking).

åḳwü', nest, leaves twisted, denotes that protected by mwọ.

ẵkwukwu (Al.), side.

ålẵ', breast, breast milk.

ålẵ, yam sp.

ålằ ọii (A), madness.

alaja, sole of foot.

alamukboko, miscarriage (animal).

ala mukpoko, grass sp.

alănda, flat.

alankpo, swelled face.

alankpoku (Okp.), kid born dead.

alansăka, careless.

alefŭlu, a white yam.

alęle, hopping game.

álélé, snake.

alęte, swallow.

álĭ, worm sp. ; parasite (?)—
    (in ear, ękumafǫ).
    in eye, ali (ainya).
    in hand, ali aka.

alia (=aiya'), plates, etc.

alibǫ, plantain (powdered).

alimi iręne, crane.

alitu, yam species, grown at waterside.

álό, biting.

ålŏ, bell.

ąlŏ, understanding an argument, arrangement.

ålŏ', forbidden thing or act—
    omel' álò, he has done a forbidden thing.

àlǫ, medicine to cool body.

alǫji, yam, moderate-sized.

alolo, yam stick (small).

ålŏlŏ (O), dirt (in water).

ålŏlŏ (O), tree.

álulu, not known (person)—
    ome ǫdafi alulu, he is rich but people don't know it.

åmå (O), time, measure.

amádi, name of dance.

ámălá (oji), cloth from down river.

ămålå, action.

åmălå (ainyase), towards (evening).

 åmălå, cross beam, covered with earth.

ămȧlȧ (O), favour.

ằmȧlȧ, paddle (O).

amala, almost.

amalaju, seeing things go round (in pirouet).

amanĭa (nya, eči), at the same time.

X̌mȧ ụ̣kwụ̣ (O), step.

amazi (Obo.), magic against sickness.

amẹlẹle (O. O), charity.

ȧmữ, vertical mark on forehead or chest.

ȧmụ̣, laugh.

ȧmụ̣ iru ẹze, false laugh.

X̌múmȧ, disease, child's, of head.

X̌múmȧ, prophet.

ȧmữmȧ (O), lightning.

ằmwȧ', spleen, inflammation of.

ằmwȧ, laying information.

(onye) amwa, informer.

X̌ṅȧ, cane, rope.

X̌nabwa, bracelet (twisted), anklet.

anase ife, evening star.

anaši oba, tree sp., that won't burn.

anata, Orion's belt.

anẹ, porcupine.

anẹni (O), taking share before elder.

ani ite, bottom of pot.

(onye) ani mwadu, stranger.

ani nfe, light soil.

aninọ, easy, soft.

ani ọiča, land above flood level.

ani olu, land flooded by Niger.

ani ụnọ (O. O), verandah.

aṅkp̣alata, fish fence.

ạnogono (A), dirty ulcer.

anọgọnọgọn, quiet person, slow moving animal.

ánȯnȯ, pus, matter on sore.

ȧnúrú, store place for fish (On.).

ȧṅwú, ambush.

åpẹ̀ (? 4–2), uncircumcised boy.

åpě̀', careful, neat.

apïa, beans that have rotted (and float).

apịlịpa (O. O), loom sword.

årọ̀, year.

arọ̀, fat—

    åinyålùm årårå, I am fat.

åróró, ant.

aroro ọịča, ant.

årårå, wind (from bowels).

arụ ẹfe, chance.

    wa ṅwe arụ ẹfe imẹ̀, they can do it easily.

årụ, body, skin.

    onye arụ ẹlu ani, impatient man.

    di arụ ani, patient.

arụ nni, shivering.

arụ ọko, fever, impatience.

åsá (= asia), fish.

asama (H), ivory (bracelet).

asani (= atani) (Og.), mouse.

ase, enquiry.

asẹle, a red yam.

asẹlẹ, seed yam.

åsì, hatred.

åsì, lie.

åsì, enquiry.

asi ẹnu, ridge tree.

asia, enquiry—

    jụm asia : ask me.

åšià, yesterday's food.

ašia (I, A), wing of fowl.

åšià azụ, gills.

asïdi, girl who does not wish to marry.

asidu, pole (one point) for net.

asilẹ́, seed yam.

ašilišia, rough.

asisa, skimming (corn).

asiso ile "sweet tongue"; unreliable person.

ásǫ́, venerable.

ásó, saliva.

asokǒlo, a white yam.

àsoso, bag, narrow and long.

ạsu, poverty.

asulu ake, hunchback (person).

asunke, short.

ạ̃sụ̃sụ̃, language.

àsụ̃sụ̃, clearing bush.

àtà, palm leaf on top of wall.

átá, grass for covering house.

atǎla, niggardly.

átà ụkwụ (O), knee, back of.

atẹte, calabash cover.

ati (ainya), matter in corner of eye.

àtó, bush cow.

àtó, chewing stick.

àtọ̀ (A), boil (small).

àtọ̀ (O), comparison, advice, instructions.

atola, frog.

atolo (O. O.), upright stick in obwẹbwẹ.

ạ̃toto, point where odala is attached to tree.

ạ̃toto ọinya, proud flesh in wound.

ạtulạtu, vagabond.

atulẹtu, dirty.

awal' ainya (I A), mark in angle of eye or round eye.

awani, he goat, cut goat.

awansọninọ, chin mark.

awẹli, creeper used for making ngo.

ạ̀wǒ, sheaf.

awobi, stupid.

awoka, iguana (does not hear unless you whisper).

ạ̃wowa (Ub.), alose in the fields.

ạwu, bundle (of beans).

awụdu, a white yam.

ạ̃wụ̃ká', lizard.

ạzȧ, small thing.

åzȧ, treasure house, store of cowries.

àzaga, (fowl), feathers standing up.

azą̃ma, gaff; wood to kill fish.

azana (Ub.), boar.

azanọmwọ (Al.), one of two sections in to which Ala town is divided.

azile, widow's neck cotton (Obul.).

azịli, small hole (in pot).

àzîzȧ, answer.

àzîzȧ (A), broom.

aziza ojuku, "broom" on cap of ẹze.

azŏa, first room.

azụ, family, people behind one.

ằzụ̇, fish.

ằzụ̇', back.

àzụ̇zụ̃̇ (O), fan.

ằzụ̇zụ̇, catarrh.


B see also kb.

—ba, progressive form—

    kp̀o aja, make bricks˙; kp̀oba aja, be making bricks.

bȧ, be broken.

ba (?4), be opportune—

    obibia n̄kei ȧbȧ, your coming is opportune.

ba îlė, show power.

ba (n') ọlu, be useful.

ba n' ife, be useful.

ba na nzu, "go into chalk."

ba n' oba, increase.

baba, (market) be open.

baba (na mili), soak.

baba ụ̌čiči, become dark.

bačali, bark.

bačapu agbubo, bark.

badolu m̄ba, threaten.

baka, be opportune.

bakọ, enter—

    (in plu.) enter together.

bali, empty itself—

    akƀa abali, the basket is empty.

bami, enter deeply, get worse.

ban' ofu ọlu, work alone.

bawa, burst.

bazili, correct, explain well.

be, (O). home, house.

bè, stop flying.

bê, to perch.

bé, to call.

bẽ, to cut, etc.

be mbubu, cut the calabash (in magic).

be n' oḳu, leave message unsaid.

be uče, cut with circumcision knife.

bẹbe ṅwunye, engage wife.

bẹdo ṅwunye, engage wife.

bedobe, climb tree by cross-sticks.

bẹkata, cry continually.

bẹkwasi (trs.), lean.

bẹnụ (O.O), diminish.

benyelu oḳu, talk in turn.

bẹtu, cut down (corn).

bi, press, print.

bị̃, be calm.

bí, to stay.

bi, to touch.

bia dẹbe, come near.

biakute, come near, meet.

biali (adj.) soft.

biali, come regularly.

biambiam, share.

    mbwaka ṅwe biambiam, I get share with you.

bičibe, be neighbours.

bičiê ụnọ, take care of house (after death).

bičie ụzọ, build house on road.
bie ọko, bring fire.
bikwali, beg.
bili, respect.
bilikwa, (H) beseech.
binie, stand up.
bite ọko, big fire.
bó, accuse, wear, help up with.
bọ', give present (to dancer).
bọ, force open (eyes or soft thing).
bọ̀, pay out.
bọ́, scratch, be black and white.
bọ (ji), dig yams (2nd time).
bọ abọ' (Uk), seize.
bo ofu ogoli, accuse.
bó' ebubo asi, accuse falsely.
bó' nankiti, accuse falsely.
bọ kiti kiti, splash over (of boiling water).
bọ́ mbọ, take revenge.
bọ ịñbọ̀, try to discover.
bọ mpi, find by enquiry.
bọ ọbọ, avenge.
boa, bark.
boa, spit.
bobwọ iyi, retract oath.
boči ọnụ, calumniate.
bọgọnite (sun, moon), rise.
bọka mbọ, try to know all.
bokwasi ísi, win (in game).
bọni abọni, dig out (yams).
bopụ, spit, remove from mouth.
bọpụta, dig up yams second time (without roots).
bosi, put off (clothes).
bota ọ́sa, (O), bring home wanderer.
bu ạinyạ̀, hide by the way.
bú, carry, be hot.
bũ, make large.

bu, glitter.

bụ̈, hatch.

ɓú, plant.

bụ̈, powder coarse meal (with stick).

bú, ride—

 bú ainyinya, ride a horse.

bụ̀, to be.

ɓu (akṗo) grow (cassava).

ɓu (ji), plant, grow (yams).

bụ̀ (n̄kẹm), be (mine)—

 obụga n̄kem, it has been mine.

bụ (ọǰa), blow (flute).

(afifia) ɓụ aɓụ, shed leaves.

bu aiya, fight.

bu ákwá luz' ụnọ (I.A), have connection with stranger (end of widow's mourning).

mwa bu… (3rd p.), stumble, fall.

bụ̈ abụ (boa (ǎbó)), sing.

bu awai ọku (talk indistinctly).

bu ẹ̈ji (Ub.), sacrifice to ancestors.

bụ̈ ẹkbai (As.), be priest.

bu ẹ̀kɓá, be lazy.

bụ̈ íbụ̀, be stout.

bu iru, be angry; turn away face.

bụ m̀bụ̀ (3rd. p.) hurt.

bu na nana, (lamp) be bright.

bu ńzọ take widow.

ɓu ọčo, murder.

bu ọfịfi, whistle.

bu' ọnụ, blow (in cursing).

bụ́ ọnụ, curse.

bú uka, (A), be fierce, ? make noise, be angry.

bu nruru (O), run (liquid).

bubwe (igari), mix into paste.

bučali nạnẹ̈we, spy on, watch from hiding place.

bučali nẹne, hide and look at p.

ɓučasi, finish killing.

buči ụzọ, close road.

bude, put down (load).

bude n'ani, put near ground.

di budu, thick (oil).

buę, kill.

buę, carve (knife and mallet)—
    ẹbulum akẹka, I carved (a door).

bue ani, flood (the land).

bue ukbo, (many) fight (one).

buga, carry to.

bugali ảinyả, note, perceive with eye.

bugạli ảinyả, make hiding place by way.

bugodu isi, be first.

buji ani, cut down trees.

buke (fire), shine.

buke, cut off piece.

bukọba, collect.

buli n'iku, make facial sign.

bụli bụli, shining like small stones on the ground.

bulu ani (water) cover land.

bulu ịkp̀a, be poor.

bulu bulu, seldom.

bulute, go to meet.

buluzida, had it been—
    buluzida n'abiam, ntam bubu ife, if I had come, I
        should have done (s).

buna iyi, retract oath.

buni (ẹnu), lift up.

bunita, lift up.

bunye ọiya, infect, communicate infection.

bupu, cut off.

bupue, bore hole.

buso aɣa (aiya), war against.

bụta ọsọ, come upon a runaway.

bute, carry home.

bute oḳu, cause palaver.

buto, cut down.

buwute, carry gladly, with all one's strength.

bwå, bind, be big, reach.

bwá, run, scrape, make, war, wrestle, sting, get fat, divine,
    be empty, tell secret, etc.

bwa, skin.

bwa, cover (goat) (quadruped).

bwa, grow big, be gravid.

bwa, bend.

bwa;—azi bwaii, be lazy (to one who threatens, so that he
    may do nothing).

bwa (ṅkpese), take (title).

bwa ababa (Id. U.), bring gifts before recognition as suitor.

bwa abụ, open abscess.

bwá abwa (come, etc.), crackle (on fire).

bwà abwa, spring up (corn).

bwa adaru, tie up crooked.

bwa ainya, spy.

bwa ainya mili, weep.

bwa ainya ačiči, dazzle.

bwa aji, grow hair (on body).

bwa akpa, play with broken calabash.

bwa akwa, make fringe to cloth.

bwa apẹ', be few (3rd p.).

bwa azi, (1) eat; (2) speak, get no reply (in morning).

bwa dim, keep silence.

bwa ẹbo, tell story of the ẹbo (to child).

bwa ẹgo, (1) thread cowry armlet; (2) count money; (3)
    account for money.

bwa ẹkwẹnsu, dance, etc., at Ekwensu.

ẹzi bwa, menstruate.

bwa ibilibi, be wild (and intend to do harm).

bwa ifilifi (1) be very big; (2) puzzle.

bwa ikbẹle mili, walk by side of water.

bwá ilẹle, crackle.

bwa iru mwọ (O.O), bring offerings for mwọ (suitor)

bwa ịta play for wages.

bwa iwunẹ (1) surprise; (2) hesitate.

bwa iyi, bind with oath.

bwa izu, take council.

bwa kpoi, make noise.

bwà mwanu, produce oil.

bwa mbia, go travelling (doctor).

bwa mbọ strive, try to find out.

bwa mili, give water to child.

bwa mme, bleed.

bwa na, kick at.

bwa ṅge, spy, watch, listen.

bwa ngẹlẹgọ, evade, walk round.

bwa ṅgo, reckon bride price.

bwa nje, run to and fro.

bwá nnu, spit salt on ground, swear.

bwá (ụkụ) n'okute, strike against stone.

bwa nrịra, cohabit outside house, take friend (wife of
    ? impotent husband by whom she does not conceive).

bwaje ọsọ, run fast.

bwaka, cut (cloth).

bwaka abwakọ, be growing, (and not full grown).

bwa nti okọ, call p. aside to tell s.

bwa ụnọ, tie fence, house.

bwa of a (k.), be stout.

bwa ose aka, wander (without work).

bwa n' ụzọ, knock at the door.

bwa ṅwuba, keep eyes half shut.

bwa ṅwuba iru, frown.

bwa obọ', tune guitar.

bwa ọčiči, be dark.

bwa odïbo, wait on.

bwa ogige, fence.

bwa oinya (Al.), set trap.

bwa ọko, buy in a hurry.

bwa ọko, be burnt.

(ọko) bwa ụnọ (house), burn—

    ọko bwalu ụnọ, the house is burnt.

bwa ọkwa (of woman), commit adultery.

bwaọsọadaru, run round; run to place at back by other road.

bwa'ọ tọlo, remain unsettled.

bwa tọpụ, loose (rope).

bwa ụbẻ (On), stab.

bwa udu, talk nonsense.

bwa ụka, be sour.

bwábǎ, run.

bwaba na nkọnu (food), go wrong way.

bwabẹbe (trs.), lean.

bwabolo, run to meet.

bwabu, kill.

bwấbụ, speak ill of it in song.

bwača, own, get (property).

bwǎčỉ, be cloudy.

bwačiẹte, run back; buy back (slave).

bwači ụzọ, close road.

bwada, descend.

bwado, hold a pawn.

bwado abwado, tie faggot.

bwado abwado, be wicked to.

bwado ainya, fix eye, persevere.

bwado nkṕologwugwu, take root.

bwadoba iru, frown.

bwadugbe iru, make angry face, pretend anger.

bwafo, be cloudless, clear.

bwafụ (ta), run out; redeem.

bwagọba (ọpia) bend cutlass.

bwaiale, astonish.

bwaiali, abandon.

bwaiali, neglect, forsake.

bwǎinye, pour in.

bwaiya (obị ẹgo), change, exchange.

bwaiya abwaiya, contradict.

bwakali (afọ), grow out of s. (e.g., enlarged stomach); grow more thin.

bwakằntỉ, piquant, sharp, bitter, sour.

b̃wakạntî, disagreeable (to ear).

bwakili ani, run to and fro.

bwakọba, meet (intr.)

bwạkp̀o izu, plot, hold secret meeting.

bwaku (ama), prove (act).

bwakwndo, run to meet (p.)

bwakwu (aka), crack (fingers).

bwalu abwalu, change to bad ; stir and make dirty.

bwalu ọji, taste kola.

bwamalẹ̈je, mosquito larva.

bwanare, winner of race.

bwankiti, ant, winged, comes after rain, drops wings.

bwanyụ, pour out (with water).

bwape, cut crooked.

bwapẹbe, cut in pieces.

bwaru, flow.

—mme. run blood.

bwasapụ, spread wings.

bwaso, follow.

bwatia aka, run far.

bwatọ, leave in disgust.

bwaṭo okụ, tell secret.

b̃watu, shoot down.

bwawa, shell (beans).

bwawali, graze (missile) ; cut off price.

bwayalayala, disorder.

bwazili, give good advice.

b̃ue, kill, tire.

bwẽ, mix.

bwe (na mili), soak.

arụ bwẽ, be tired.

bwe ẹbwẹ, tie in small parcels.

bwe ịbwe, crawl (child), move stealthily.

bwẹbe, creep—

   ẹ́bwẹ̀bẹ̀m, I am creeping.

bwẹbe, mix—

   ẹ̣bwẹ̣bẹ̣m, I am mixing.

bwębu, soil.

Ƃwe fusie, clear altogether.

bwęle, loiter, creep.

bwęlia ǫlụ, work too much.

bwenye n'arụ, neglect, play the superior person.

bwępu, very bad (smell).

di bwidi, thick (oil).

bwǫ́, moo, etc.

bwó, in time—

    abiarǫm bwo, I come late.

bwodo, very flat.

bwǫli, long ago.

bwǒlǒlǒ, not spreading (of tree); tall and thin.

bwụ̃, remain over.

bwo, wear (on body).

bwo (ogęde), grow bananas.

bwo (okbęte), grow sugar cane.

bwo arụ, get thin.

bwo ṅkpa, relieve.

bwo ṅkpa, prevent from desiring.

bwo ofufu, foam.

bwǫ osisi, plant tree.

bwǫ ụzǫ, stop p. from passing.

bwobido (mili), stop (water).

bwoči (mili) stop water.

bwodo agụ, satisfy hunger.

bwǫfǫ, remain over.

bwǫ nyụ (water), put out (unintentionally).

bwụpụ, take off clothes.

bwụ, shed leaves.

Ƃwú', kill—

    oƃuenye, he kills it.

    bueƃue, kill it.

Ƃwú', blow (instrument).

Ƃwú', plant.

bwụ, cover, check, stand, stop, remain over.

Ƃwu (akụ), cut (nuts).

b̕wụ (mbwu), cut down trees (big) in farm.
bwu (mbwu), distress.
b̕wu ẹbwubwu, cut marks.
bwu fifia, flash.
bwu inyẹge inyẹge, glisten, shine but not clear.
bwuča, cut side, clip hedge.
bwuča, shed leaves (yams).
bw·ụča abwụča, slip, be slippery.
bwudo ainya, persevere, remark.
bwudo isi, dress hair, do hair roughly.
b̕wufo, hack way through.
b̕wuǰipu, break, cut off.
b̕wuǰira, cut in half.
b̕wụlụ, stop.
b̕wụpụ, cut off; glitter.
b̕wutu, cut down.
b̕wuwa ụzọ, cut new road.


čá, be ripe, wash, be red.
čä̆, be too clever.
čá, scorch.
č ạ̈, give place.
ča ilẹ, lose strength.
čå n 'ụzọ, get out of the way.
čaba, (sun) shine.
čaba, be ripe; dazzle.
čåbå, get out of the way.
čaba, wait for—
　　ñčabåli, can I wait for you.
čabali, seize person unexpectedly.
čabe, stop scorching.
čab̕ue, scorch up.
čab̕ue oinya, heal sore.
čača, gamble.
čạde, (fruit) become over soft.
čaka čaka, a little (palm wine) (O. O).

čalu, become (over) soft (fruit).

čakp̣u obi, bend over.

čaru (iru), change colour.

čaya, become (over) soft (fruit).

čayẹsie, be over ripe.

čé, grind (beans) or ground.

čé (čé n̄čé), watch—
   ẹ́čẹ̀m n̄čẹ̀, I watch.

čë, groan, pant in childbirth.

čẹ̀, think.

čé, watch.

čẹ̀ ùčẹ̀, change mind—
   èčẹ̀m ùčẹ̀m, I change my mind.

čẹ̀bẹ̀, think.

čẹbido, stop person, make person halt.

čẹdo, take thought for.

čẹko arụ, be in early stage of pregnancy.

čẹkunie (Al.), trust.

čeya, think again.

čị́, take (pl. object)—
   cị́ mwọ, take nze (as ọkpala).

čí (mwọ), take title.

či, roll seed to husk it.

čị́, rule over.

čị̃, chirp.

čị̣, shut.

čí, screw, turn.

čị̃, rub.

čí nzu, rub chalk.

či oči, bleed, suck blood—
   ẹ̀čîm òčị̂, I bleed someone.

či (a) daba, 6.0 p.m.

či (e) fobe, 5.0 a.m.

či (e)fočẹ, 8.0 a.m.

či (e)fonata, 4.30 a.m.

či (a)golo, 3.0—4.0 p.m.

či (e)ǰibe, 5.30—6.0 a.m.

či (e)ĵiẹ, 12.0 p.m.

či (a)ĵimi go, 2.0 a.m.

či (e)ĵiri, 6.0—6.30 p.m.

či (e)ĵitẹ, 12.0 p.m.

či (ẹ)kufo, 5.30 a.m.

či (a)kṗodafu, 4.0 p.m.

èi (a)loa, be afternoon, 4.0 or 5.0 p.m.

či (ẹ)mie, 12.0 p.m.

èi (a)na, be past midday (1.0—2.0 p.m. ?).

èi (a) nǎ, 4.0—5.0 p.m.

či (e) rulu, be afternoon, 4.0 or 5.0 p.m.

či (e) runẹte, 5.0—6.0 p.m.

čị očị, withdraw something offered.

čịbe, put, place firmly—

    čib' ite, set the pot right.

(ĵe) čibe, go near.

čịdẹbe, bring near.

čiẹ, return—

    ndụm ẹčiẹ, my life returns.

čịkoba, gather.

čịkonyesia, gather and give all.

čịkọta, gather all.

čikwapo, dislocate.

čịnia aka, be free, innocent.

čịpu, take (small things) away.

čịta, take money from brother of debtor—

    ečitẹmi, I take money from you.

čịtọ (n'ani), put (many).

čὸ, display for sale.

čǫ́, want, look.

čὸ ákwá, tell bad news.

čọ iyi, go for water.

čọ k' ọkubẹpu, (stop) be at point of death.

cọ okụ cause palaver.

čobe, take fire—

    ọko ačobe, fuel is taking fire.

čὸbe, expose for sale (corn, salt, fish).

čǫ čo, die in person's hand.

čǫfe, seek round about.

čǫputa, search out.

čǫsa, search everywhere.

čǫta oku, cause palaver.

čụ, drive, offer.

čụ' aǰa, sacrifice.

čụ aǰụ, make giddy.

čụ ǫbwakulo, throw fire in Niger.

čụ ǫko, run (liquid) (A).

čụ olǫ, throw fire in Niger.

ču uču, try hard.

čụ ụla be sleepless.

čụ ụlǫ, exorcise by fire.

čụsa scatter.


då, fall, pain, be moist, be difficult—

    ife nadam, what is hard for me to get.

dá, press down, bump.

då ådå, fall down.

dá (ofe) ádå, warm up soup.

då aka, lay hands on.

da añwu, lie in wait.

da ịkpa become poor.

da isi, consult.

da mbuba, keep secret.

då nańkǫ, fall on one side ; sit on one side.

då nyoi, be silent, say no more.

då n' aka, take by hand.

då nra, fine, ask to pay.

då n'ụkwụ, happen in presence of, fall on the foot.

da obwei, become poor.

da obǫsi, fix a day.

da ǫda, requite on s. brother—

    ǰi nwannea adali ǫda, to take a brother for vengeance.

da ubwo (ainya), be hollow-eyed.

daba, begin ; fall in.

daba (ofe), put (soup) on fire.

dabainye, fall into.

dačali, stagger.

dabęli, (tr) lean.

dači (ụzọ), (tree) block road.

dadạlida, daily.

dado, lean against, push.

dayali, leave, lying.

dakępu, die.

dakpo, fall upon—

   ani adakpom tata, the earth fell on me to-day. (I have too heavy a burden.)

dakolu, stick, be suspended.

dakpudo, fall on (and cover).

dalu (A), thank you, good morning.

dalua, try.

dami, test, try.

danari, fall from.

danda, yellow house ant.

dawusa, fall on.

dawụzọ, fall straight, happen well.

dé, rumble, write, touch.

dẹ̈, melt, think (?), wait, wet.

dé (akwa), iron, press cloth.

de ẹde, grow (corn) yams.

dẹ̈ ẹde, be very smooth.

dẹ ile, dip finger and taste.

de inyẹle, grunt, murmur.

dé iru, draw lines on face—

   ẹ̈dẹ̈m iru, I draw lines.

dé ụdẹ̈, be famous.

dẹbe ọnụ dú, be silent.

dẹbe uče, think, keep in mind.

dečapu, cancel.

dẹču, wash new cloth.

defie, spell wrong.

dẹfu ndo, be still alive.

dejẹ (A), thank you.

dẹka, break by ironing.

dẹka, write and (1) break pen; (2) tear paper; (3) reach hole
    in paper.

dekaka, rub all over.

dèlẹdẹ (A), soft food.

deli (A), thank you.

deliteli, correspond (by letter).

dẹme (A), thank you.

dẹpu, wet through.

dị, to be—

    adịlim ndo, I am well.

    arụ adẹrọa, he is ill.

    arụi dịkwọ mma, are you well?

    arụ dịli unu, are you well?

dị ime, be pregnant.

dị ka, just like.

    ọdimka, I think.

dị n' ainya, desire, like.

dị na nkọ, lie on one side.

dị ńdò, be alive.

dị ńdò ibe, be sick, half alive, dangerously ill.

dị n' ife, be useful.

dị ńkpà, be necessary.

dị ńkpằ', be few.

dị n' obi, be dear, be in mind.

dị ntitia, be shameful.

dị n' uru mwaka, mourn.

dị nyạla, favour, be on p. side.

dị nyẹli, favour, be on p. side.

dị ọgọ, be grateful.

dị oke ọnụ, be costly.

dị odọ, be short, scanty.

dị tasi, lose sense of taste—

    ile dịm tasi, I can't taste it.

dị tili, lose sense of taste.

di ùnù, be in a hurry—
  ije dim ùnù, I am in a hurry.
di, husband, friend.
dï, sink, endure.
ume, ike, diazi, be powerless—
  ume n' obi adiazi ya, he is powerless, breakless.
diba (ndo), begin to live.
dibeli (3rd p.), get better.
dide obi, feel nausea.
didebe, be near.
dido obi, be patient.
díkǎ, not.
dika eči, about to-morrow.
dikpọ, be like, be as big as.
dilili, continue.
dilili (ndo), be still alive.
dimi, be out of reach.
dimwọ, man entitled to give ṅkpese to his umunna.
dita ndo, be alive still.
dọ̈, give advice.
dọ́ [dua], pierce, yell.
dọ́, pull, draw blood.
dó, push, pack, pawn.
dọ̈, think, convalesce.
dọ́ okpọ̌lọ, haul in the rope of the ikum.
dọ́' n' aya, take captive.
dọ́' akainya, toil, suffer.
dọ́' akpili, long for.
dọ́' dọlidọ, pull against each other.
dọ́' ndo, haggle, be stubborn.
dọ́' nti, admonish.
dọ ụgwọ, demand payment.
dọ n' ani, sit down—
  dọ n' okbokolo, sit down on the seat.
dọ', juice, prick.
dọ' aka, point, touch.
dọ ọdọ, give advice.

dó' ani, settle a land, take care.

dó' iru, turn face towards, face.

dó n' isi, touch p. forehead.

dó' ǫdo, make place for sitting.

dŏ̆, aim at.

do ędo, (? dŏ̆) be smooth, clear ; walk quietly ; take time.

do, perplex—

    ife adędo ǫka edo obodi, what does not perplex the wise
      man perplexes the fool.

do ndo, keep long, stay long.

do odido, creep up to.

    awǫlǫ nę do anų odido, the leopard creeps up to the
      animal.

dó ojuñe, not to salute (enemy).

do ǫko, (intr.), burn.

dǫ̀, a salutation.

dǫ́ ùtè (doa ùtè), touch person with stick for divination.

dǫba, put down ; pull.

dobe n'isi, put under pillow.

doči, close (opening).

doči ųzǫ, (barrier) close road.

dǫdo, pull by arm.

dǫdǫdǫlidǫ, very long.

dǫ jue, be full moon.

dǫka, make (stubborn, etc).

dǫka anu, tear.

dǫka nnini, be stubborn.

dǫkali, tear in pieces.

dǫ́kpųkpy, draw out.

dokwa, make peace, arrange, decorate.

dokwaba isi, dress hair.

dǫkwębe, keep well.

dokwu oķu, settle palaver.

dǫli (Al.) dǫlo, pull (and drag other man, e.g. tug of war).

dolo, put (kola) on forehead—

    wa ji oru doloa n'isi, they take a slave and touch his
      head (i.e., offer slave).

dolu arụ ani, take time over.

dọna, sit.

dọna adọna, sit.

dọpụ, draw out.

doputa, come out (many).

dọputa, draw out.

dọro, tired.

doru ẹli, turn over.

dọta, acquire by toil.

dowụzo, put straight.

dozi, arrange.

dozu, complete.

dú, to lead.

(ọko) dụ...... (intr.) burn—

   ọko adụ ọzala, fire burns the bush.

dụ aja, build wall.

du ndudu ile, contradict p. who is above one.

du...... zido (ite), help down with.

du, very bad (smell).

dů, still, quiet.

dụ, calm.

dụm, all.

dune arọ (As.), " send the old year back."


e, sign of negative—

   emẹ ife, doing nothing.

ẹbà', verandah.

ẹ̀bå, rebuke.

ẹbafu, there.

ẹbala (Al.), open space (impluvium) in house.

n'ẹbe, while.

ẹ̀bě', place, where.

ẹ̀bẹ̀, caterpillar (?) that eats yam leaves, corn, etc.

ẹ̀bě (? 1–4), sling.

ẹbea, here.

ẹ̀bî, fish sp. (eats itself from its tail to its middle, then dies).

èbì, porcupine.

èbì, storm.

ẹbi (As.) feather cap of orhene.

ẹbili, wave, tornado.

ẹbili (Al.), granary.

ẹ̀bǒ, quarter.

ẹ̀bǒ, accusation.

ebo, man who finds a 'thief.

ẹbobọ iyi, recalling curse.

ẹbọwa, snake skin drum.

ẹ̀bǔbẹ̀, starving.

ẹ̀bǔbẹ̀ ? fungus (used for soup ; from felled tree).

èbǔbè, fear.

ẽ̀bǔbǒ (false) accusation.

ebubu imi, line down nose.

ẹbunọ, hornet, black.

ẹbu ọnụ, curse.

ẹ̀bwǎ' (Al.), fan palm.

ẹ̀bwã̌ ; bark cloth.

ẹbwači, woman who has borne 3–4 children (As).

ẹ̀bwạka, being empty, cracking fingers.

ẹbwanaka, putting something on hand or arm.

ẹ̀bwẹ̀, garden egg.

ẽ̀bwẹ̀, gun.

ẹ̀bwè, deserted.

ẹ̀bwè, tree.

èbwè' edge of roof.

ẹ̀bwẹ̀, hawk (fowl).

ẹbwẹbwe (Ub.), lip.

ẹbweni, fly sp.

ẹbwẹ n'ụbọsi (O), every day, always.

ẹbwẹ̃ši, useless.

ẹ̀bwǐ, antelope (? cob species).

ẹ̀bwǒ, portion of work.

ẹ̀bwõfeǒ, cracking fingers.

ẹ̀dǎ, post, pillar.

ẹde, not yet.

ẹdẹge, big belly.

ẹdẹle, mate, companion.

ẹ́di, no (that shall never be done).

ẹdide, poison.

ẹdọ, net.

ẹ̀dò, mineral (red) from stream.

ẹdolo, horn of viper.

ẹ̀fi, fish (kind of).

ẹfifie, morning, 9.0 a.m.—2.0 p.m.

ẹ̀fú, at all.

ẽfú, lie.

ẹfulẹfu, vagrant.

ẹ̀gå, molar.

ẹ̀gå, division between idumu ; two lines of ẹbwo (if cut=sign of fight).

ẹgabọ, marks under eyes (semicircular).

ego (O. O), cowry, they count cowries by two to twenty.

ẹgo aiyọlọ, small cowries (As), worth twice as much as big

ẹgọlọ, shin.

ẹ̀gù, fear.

ẹ́gù, danger.

ẹ̀gǔ, dance.

ẹ̀gù (O), drum.

ẹgu igoši, fear (caused by amụzụ) ; fear (child's).

ẹ̀gwé' (O), wall round compound.

ẹ̀gwẹ́, hoe.

ẹgwẹle, bird sp., small.

ẹgwọta (As), burial dance.

ẹ̌jaǰa, disease that makes one shiver (five minutes).

eǰakpa, fly whisk.

ẹ̌ji (Ub), snail species.

ẹ̀ǰò (O), fish species.

ẹ́ǰǔ, potsherd.

ony ẹka, some one.

ẹkbá, lazy.

ẹkba (O), box.

ẹkbaịčalaịnya (O), purposely (he takes care).

ǝkɓale amu (A), game.

ękɓ̀ę̀', yam species.

ękɓ̀ę̀ loopholed wall (on farm to keep cows).

ękɓe (O), time.

ę́kɓè (O), pit for animal, or in war.

ękɓęde (O), crossbow.

ękɓęke (A), shield (wicker).

Ękbęli, Kukuruku.

ękbę̌lima (A), burglar, big thief.

èkɓ̌ęlu, prayer.

ękɓ̌ęrima (A), highway robber, burglar, farm thief.

ękbęte, five cowries.

ękbo, when.

ękɓó (A), help (in palaver), work together (pulling log, etc.)—

     fakbolum ękɓó, they do work together.

ękbotękbo, thick (wood).

ụ́bǫ̀sì ę̌kè̌, Eke day.

ękęlękbǫ, animal (hermaphrodite !)

ekęlęmu, informer.

ękęlęsi, straight.

ęke ǫ́bwǎ, python, 8 feet long.

ękęti, accidentally.

ękike, many-coloured (fowl).

ę́kǐkě, adornment.

ę̌kíkě ile, fraenum of tongue.

ękikó, rust.

ękili, meteor.

ękǫbwa, python sp.

ękp̀ačinti (O), obstinacy.

ękpęlęke, shaking, not in equilibrium.

ękp̀ę obwǫ, steersman.

ękp̀ǫbe (ji) (O), parcel, lot for sale.

ękp̀ụeza (A), faintness, death swoon (from hunger).

ękp̀ulękp̀u (O), blind boil (no matter) in groin ; enlarged gland in groin ; pain in groin from sore foot.

ękubu, collar bone.

ẹ̀kùmȧfọ̀, toothache, swelled face (jaw or eye).

ẹ̀kwẹ̀' drum, drumstick—
    énwèlùm ẹ̀kwǫ̀, I have a drum.

ekwele (IA), rope.

ẹkwẹnsu, "evil spirit"—
    ẹkwẹnsu aba n'ainya, an evil spirit has entered him (*i.e.*,
    he has killed someone).

ẹkwẹnsu, ekwensu dance (see **3**, 269).

ẹ̀kwó, halting place.

ẹ̀kwolo, jealousy.

ẹ̀kwulo, gate.

ẹ̀kwume, stern of canoe.

ẹ̀lái, kind (adj).

ẹle, child learning to stand.

ẹlẹbwe (nya, eči), at the same time.

ẹlẹgẹdẹ, big (tree, man, cow).

ẹ̀lẹ̀lè, food, like okbǫ.

ẹlẹndǫ̀le, top (toy).

ẹlẹntili, top made of seed.

ẹ̀lílí, snake.

ẹ̀lílí (O), tie-tie.

ẹ̀lili, electric fish.

ẹ̀lili (O), tree species.

ẹlili ụkwụ, anklet.

ẹlulǔ, ant, black, long line on road.

ẹmu (Og), sickness.

ẹ̀ne, innocent—
    ẹlilịm ẹne, I am innocent.

ẹnẹke, swift (bird).

ẹni, unkind.

ẹnu ani, high land, hinterland.

ẹnu ọlilǫ, untroubled life.

ẹ̀nwè, monkey (ènwè, has)

ènyì, disease.

ènyì, friend (sexual).

ènyǐ, elephant.

ènyi (Al.), target.

enyi, itching in pregnancy.

ènyọ̄, senseless.

ènyó, grass sp., grows near river.

ẹra, people.

èrì, since.

èrì mbweafu, since then.

èrì ọ́kpụ̀. ever since.

ẹrigúnne', big—

    ǹwåtå ẹ̀rîgụ̀nẹ̀', the child is big.

ẹrimodo (On), ešimodo, grasshopper.

ẹsani, esanọ, boil, sore formed after swelling.

ẹ̀sẽ, enquiry—

    ìjụ̀èsè (A), asking doctor.

    ặčụ̊åm ẹ̀sẹ̀, I look for a quarrel.

    mùnyå nẹ̀sẹ̀ ẹ̀sẹ̀m ôkù, he and I have a quarrel.

èsù, millipede.

(onye) ẹsu, unlucky.

êsù alose;—otọ, kind of millipede.

esubwoko, bush millipede.

esuǹwali, black millipede.

ètå, lot.

ẹ̀tẽ, target.

ẹ̀tẽ, climbing rope [ẹ́tẽ, to rub].

ẹ̀tè, offence.

ẹtili, medicine against knife ; trembling ;

    ẹtili awu kpom—takes hold of me.

eṭòinu, proverb.

éṭọlà (O), ruse.

ètọǹkwọ̀' (A), three things piled on one

ètù, leech.

ètù', sort, kind, colour, shape.

ẹtu ọfo (O), such as.

ẹtum, open sand (or land).

eṭụṭụ̣, paying tax.

ẹwa irhu, face marks.

ewi (Og., At., Is.), giant rat.

ẹwo, fresh.

ẹwu n'awọlọ, good and bad (also mwado na mwọ).
ẹwu oiyi (Ib.), goat sent to girl who refuses to go to husband.
ẹwữči, goat given by suitor to girl.
èyì, giant rat.
ĕzẹ́, tooth.
ẹ̀zẹ̀, priest, king.
ẹze ẹlili, healthy stock (parents or children).
ẹze ogẹde, red plantain.
ẹzẹne, ordinary wives (not ọmaku).
ézẹne, man with many wives—
    ọbwa ẹ́zẹne, he has many wives.
ẹze soaii, end post of ikum.
ẹzi, also.
ĕzì, pig.
ĕzì, road.
ẹ̀zì, menstruation, menstrual blood.
ẹ̀zĭ, eaves, under (outside house).
ẹ́zi imi, blood from nose.
ẹzi obulu, centre opening of house.
ẹzibo, kind, true, very.
ẹ̀zìòkừ, truth.
ezubwo (As), head of the ọbwọ; holds position for ten years.


fằ, shout.
fá, to wedge.
fá' na oṅwefa, they themselves.
fači, close (with leaf).
fado, stuff.
faṅwa, they.
fapụ, ease, take away.
fé', sprinkle, cast.
fé', revive—
    ẹ̀fẹ̀m mwadu, I revive a man.
fé, cross over.

fé, fly, jump, visit.

fé ainyike (Uk), sharpen axe.

fé (isi), shake (the head).

fé obwodo, go round the town.

fé ụzo, leave road (purposely).

fẽ, serve—

   èfèm, I serve.

fe nru, pay dues.

fé oke, surpass.

fẹ, the whole.

fẹba, fly into.

fẹde, swoop down on (hawk).

féfẹga, fly across.

fẹfẹlẹfẹm, not at all.

fẹfu, fly away.

fẹpụ, release fowl for purification.

fẹgo, fly up.

feɣali, fly about.

feji, (wind) break in two.

fẹkasi, break by shaking.

fẹli aka, wave the hand.

fẹnaba, fly home.

fẹné ẹfẹné, fly into home.

fẹnẹ̀ ẹfẹnẹ̀, examine.

fẹni, fly up.

fẹniri, fly up.

fẹṅwụ, wither.

fenye, fly into.

fẹpụ, blow away, fly away.

fẹrube, pass round.

fẹrube, wave, shake.

fẹsa oku, tell tract.

fẹsi, sprinkle.

feši (igwé), clear up.

fešigo, be tired, dying—

   umeya ẹfẹšigo, he is tired, dying.

fetaba, begin to come, fly.

fẹtẹ, visit.

fẹtẹbẹ, begin to come, fly.

fetọ ẹfetọ, be twisted.

fẹwosi, sprinkle.

fi, be firm.

fị, screw, turn.

fi', form, boil, press, rub hard, crush, wipe by pressing.

fí (isi), support (the head).

fí ẹkbẹlẹke, shake (Ob).

fí erube, bind all round.

fĭ, cut lightly.

fĭ, pass hand over eyes.

fĭ ainya, look different.

(iru) fie, (face) changes ; is not straight.

fi ọla, slap.

fịa afia, flatten.

fịa ọfifia, encourage (of sick p. ; *e.g.*, ask to get up and walk).

fiača, shake out dust.

fibĕ, put in position.

  fib odo, place the mortar.

fičĕ (arụ), rub (body), towel.

fido, fix, make steady.

fie, miss.

  ẹfiẹ m, I miss.

fie, be infectious.

fie akwa, put on cloth without tying.

fie ṅgo, receive back brideprice (H).

fie ụgwọ, seize for debt—

  ejim ẹfie ụgwọ ; ẹfiẹm, I seize for debt.

fiebwado, tie.

fiẹdo iwu, keep law.

fiekọnata (ibn), lighten (load).

fielya, tie so that string cuts in.

owa fienerhi (onye), be a failure (Uk).

fienẹši, disappear (game).

fiẹnẹno, feel weak.

fiẹpụ, loose.

fiẹpụ, fall (unripe fruit).

fieta (H), receive back bride price.

fifi, swell.

fifi afifi, twist, coil.

fifie, wave wood (as torch), wave hand to stop p.

fime, astonish.

fịnata, lower (lamp).

fịnite, screw up (lamp).

finite, help p.

fió, (heart) beat (whip) crack.

fiọputa (ẹze), take and took.

fịpụ, extract nail, loose screw.

fịta fịte, revive dying person.

fitọ, unfasten and put down.

fọ̈, blow.

fọ́, pack.

fọ́' ọkọkọlọ, make bunches.

fọ̈, wash head.

fó, (day) break—
    či ẹfogo, day breaks.

fó iru, be open, clear.

fó ufọ́, spread report.

fọbẹnẹtẹ (ibu), lighten (load).

fọfẹli obwa, overload calabash.

fonata, (sky) clear up, cool down.

fọpu, unpack.

fụ, see—
    afụm: I see, I saw.

fụ' inyẹge, see faintly.

fụ iru n' iru, see face to face.

fụ́ ọfụ, see visions.

fụ́ ụzọ, see clearly, see way.

fụ iru njọ, dislike.

fụ ọfụfụ, hurt.

fụ́, roll up.

fụ́ afụ, roll up.

fụ (?) akp̣a, husk (corn).

fu, very bad (smell).
fụ̈, come out.
fụ́, hurt, pinch.
fụ̈ (ụzọ), go astray—
   ọ́fụ̂, he sees.
   ôfụ̂, he loses.
fụ́' anụ, smoke animal out.
fụa puta, come out.
fụča, see clearly.
fụča obwadu, husk corn.
fụ́čie, close (mouth of bag).
fụda, see to the end ; fall down.
fụdo afụdo, have seen before.
fụ̈ efu, go astray.
fụẹli, wander abroad.
fụfụ n' ọnụ (word) stays long in mouth.
fụga, fold (twice or more).
fụǰọ, be ill-disposed.
fụǰụ, see and refuse.
fụkọ (?), roll (with hand).
fụkọba, roll together.
fụkọli iru, see face to face.
fụlě̈ (3rd p.), surprise.
fụmi, see to the bottom.
fụmu ọko, blow up fire.
funari, wander from.
fụni, roll up.
fụ̀nyụ̀, blow out.
fụnyụ, blow out.
funyǎa nto, blow up powder.
furu, be lost.
   ume furu, have no strength.
fụsi ike, fold tight.
fụ̀wǎ, puff and burst.
fụ́wá, see clearly.
fụzụ, see all.

gà, thread (beads).

gá, be prosperous, pass over, go.

gå, will (*future*).

gá ifufuge, go (without stopping), go on.

gabulu n' iru, go before.

gafe, pass over, go away.

gafẹga, go on without stopping.

gakọ, pass towards, pass.

gala ṅgala, be proud.

galawainya, become dearer.

gami, go in ; travel inland.

gana gana, one by one.

ganata, be few—

ndi afia ganata, most of the market people have gone already, those that remain are few.

garube, surround, pass round.

garuka, go aside, go on (in front).

gata, pass here, come.

gazu, pass through.

gbainyaka n' azụ, mark on back of shoulder.

gé, tie, fasten.

gé, wait, watch.

gè (ẹgẹm), listen.

gé . . . ngige, close road with cord.

gegado, tie loosely.

gẹle gẹle, seldom ; very slender.

genye, till—

čeli genye na mbia, wait till I come.

gẹwẹte fetch.

gidigidi, very much ; great noise.

gini, what.

gini mẹlu, why.

gö, be glad.

gọ́ (O), count.

gó, buy.

gọ́ agugọ, deny.

gọ agigọ, deny.

gǫ agǫ, deny.

gǫ' mbǫ, scratch.

gǫ ǫgǫ, perform duties of son-in-law.

gǫ afa, name.

gǫ ǫnụ, count.

gǫ mbasi, restore a wrong.

gó, buy corn.

gŏ, ákwá, bewail.

gó ngigo, sing.

gó' ngo, give dash to, bribe.

gočiẹte, buy back.

godẹte, come down slowly.

gogo, appease; quieten child.

gogoa, comfort.

gokwasi ísi, win (in game.)

gǫi gǫi, hammering—

    kusi gǫi gǫi, stop that hammering.

gǫlo, be crooked.

golo ali (trs). stir.

golo golo, (A), clear water.

golu, buy, hire (men).

gǫnari, deny.

gosi, buy all.

gǫsi, show.

gote (akwa), buy.

gụ, desire.

gụ, read.

gụ, count—

    agoam, I counted.

    agum, I count.

gụ ǫnụ, count—

    gụ mwadu ǫnụ, take a censor.

gụ ǫra, shine bright (sun).

gụ afa, give name.

gu, have sad countenance.

gu egu, look sad.

gu iru, pretend anger.

(onye) gu isa, chatterer.
'gu ǫbo, make yam store.
'gu ire, make yam store.
'gu (ji), dig yams, (1st time)
'gu, dig.
gu, play; swim.
gu ẹkuaba, swim on back.
guči, close.
gučiẹte, have luck.
gue ini (gwe ini), dig grave.
gųfe, make hole in wall and pass through.
gųgẹ, loosen, open.
gųgų, comfort, soothe.
'gukwudo, discover hidden object (in ground).
gųnye, add, reckon, (na, as) count.
'gupute, dig up.
gusi, unload.
gųsia, be finished.
gųtali ǫko, take fire from house of another.
gųta ǫko, bring fire.
gwa, search.
gwa ǫgu, make medicine.
gwa oku nzizǫ, tell secret.
gwagide, convince.
gwečẹ ṅgwečẹ, be impertinent.
gwẹne, mash (with foot).
gwǫ, mix with liquid.
gwǫ,' search.
gwǫ kǫba[ma] (trs.). bend.
gwǫ kǫlo, roll sleeves up.
gwǫlǫ, walk bend and knock-kneed.
gwǫ ṅgwųlǫ, be lame.
gwǫ nkuluku, coil.
gwǫ nsi, make poison.
gwǫ ǫgų, mix medicine
gwǫ ųnǫ, search house.
gwá, tell, mix.

gwǫ, beat too much, snore, cure.
gwȯ, bend.
gwụ (gụ), be finished.
gwụ́, finish.
ɣá, look back.
ɣȧ, pardon, stop.
ɣé, open mouth, tell, yawn.
ɣé, patch.
ɣé, cook, fry.
ɣǫ alo, deceive (Al).

i̡, sign of infinitive.
ibȧ, court, good room.
i̡ba (Al.), king's house.
bȧ, mark, token.
íbȧ, fever.
íbȁ̈bȧ (O), insect.
ibabwulo (Ib.), part of house.
ibȇ', pawn.
íbȇ̈, companion.
ibȩli, fly whisk (fibre).
ibelibe akwȁ̈ ǫkoko ǫica, white of egg.
ibiagwali, male slaves of obi.
ibiale, female slaves of obi (or wives).
íbȍ̈, favourite wife.
ibobo, shivering.
ibǫko, 140 cowries.
ibolo, net, used by one man.
íbů, load—
  ȯbů íbů, he carries load.
íbủ, stout—
  ǫbụl' íbủ, he is stout.
i̡bủ ísí, "swelled head."
íbubi (Og.), ceremony; the same as iwaǰi.
ibubwe, sugar ant.

ibudu, coffin.

ibuluku, trouble.

ibuma (As), cloth chest.

íbwẹgulu, palm branch (cut off).

ibwẹnu, fish species.

ịbwi, gums.

ibwó, float (wood).

ibwobwo (As.), workers (*i.e.*, companies of young men).

îbwóbwó, husks of corn.

ibwudu afia, line of market women.

ičafọ, kerchief.

ičami, 800 cowries.

ícẹ̀ (On.), ball, missile.

ičẹke ọko, live coal.

ičẹndo, deputy, regent.

(onye) iče nni, guest.

(ndi) îčiẹ́, men marked with iči.

íčủ, greedy.

ičučủ, unripe (seed fallen).

iču iču, close handed person.

ịdá' (As.), post.

ídå, dance.

idabolo, idebolo, misfortune.

idé (As. and H), plant used for making cord.

idẹbwe, spinster ; daughter assigned to " friend."

idẹdu, stupid.

idẹge idẹge, away from ground, land.

idegedege, ends of roof mat.

ídẽi (O), running water (from rain).

ịdî, swelling on top of foot.

idibwe, male of ọzọ' (O, O).

ididili, big.

idime (Ub.), titled men ; the same as olinzẹle.

idime, pit (trap).

ido, ant, brown, on trees.

idọlọmwẹ, kind of bed.

idumu, subquarter.

if' arụ, ornament.

ife ẹfifie (Ala), midday meal.

ife enunu, domestic animals.

ife gạgạ. (thing) past.

ifẹgu, plaything.

ifẹmwa, price paid to ọkpalumunna of a widow before her
2nd marriage.

ife nkili, sight.

ifẹ nru, service, due.

if' ọji (Okp.), bride price.

ife ȯtȕtȕ, blister.

ifi (Og.), forbidden actions (to women).

ifili, ufili, sign, track.

ifolo, light (shining).

ifufu, small fly.

ifulifu, crumbs; small.

igạgu, prawn (big).

igạgu, huge.

igḃo, float.

ịgili, bush rope sp. (to tie yams).

igili (oyi), shivering, gooseflesh—
igili arụ kpọm, I shivered with fright.

ígȯ̆gụẹǰuna (O), shell of snail.

igoligo = igiligo (Isẹle), air, atmosphere.

igorhi, igosi, children.

ígȕ, palm branch (on tree).

ȋgȕ, mark on abdomen.

iguakainya, leaf (bambu).

ịgugȕ, long knife, two-edged.

igulube, ? locust, grasshopper.

ȋgwȇ', sky.

ȋgwȇ oǰi, cloud.

ȋgwḝ', iron,

ịgwḝ' (O), flock, many, crowd.

igwọji, yam (sliced).

ịjakpa, fly whisk (skin).

iǰali obwẹdu, flower (of corn).

iǰęlę (Al., H.) = ęlulu, ant sp. ; driver.

iǰeli (I.A.), eight thousand.

ikale (Uk.), fruit like tomato.

ịkàmî, very old.

ịkƀa (Al.), ivory (bracelet).

ịkƀa, poor man.

ịkbámụ̀, playing, joking.

ikƀanna, greedy person (O).

ìkƀázu, last.

ìkƀ&#7869;̣, case, judge, judgment.

ìkƀê, backbiting, abuse.

ikbękęle, cake of yam, corn, beans.

ìkƀo, many.

ìkƀŏ, bell.

ìkƀŏ, grass sp.

ikƀokƀo, fish species.

ikƀokƀo, vexation.

ikbǫkǫ ozu, keeping fire on grave.

ikbŏlo, unilateral paralysis.

ịkbǫnto, rubbish heap.

ikbosu ozu (As.), day before burial of anase.

ìkƀu, dassia.

ịkƀù (Abǫ), vulva.

ìkƀù, " thorn " of nuts, bunch.

ìk ƀù, shrub sp.

ikbutu, thick.

ìkê', wasp.

ike ite, bottom of pot.

ikękwa, perhaps.

ikęle, fish trap.

ikęlike, crumbs.

ikęnę (As.), woof thread, skein, ball.

ĭkęnę (Ub.), alose in the field ; the same as ifejiǫko.

ikeṅga ǫkwa, new ikenga made by second husband.

ikęti (Ub.), vexation.

ikętu, violent, terrible (death); urgent.

n'ikili, (A), without biting.

ikilibisi, stump (of tree).

ikili ụkwụ, heel, footfall.

ịkịti, brass ornament.

ikiti, footfall.

ịkọ́, gutter.

ikoliko, thicket.

ikolo, (Ub.) workers.

ikolo anụ, (O.O), stick to guide animal to snare.

ikolŏto, ikolotu, young man.

ẹ́kp̀a, (Al.) ivory.

ikp̀asikp̀a, first fence.

ịkp̀at' ụḳwụ (A). heel.

ikp̀ẹte, rich woman.

ikp̀u ụnọ, house with many inmates.

iku (m), males of (my) family.

iku ainya, eyelashes.

iku ainya, eyelid.

ikubẹnka, ants' nest.

ïkŭkŭ, black eye.

ikwẹle, drove of pigs.

ikwẹle (Ibuzọ), dance headman.

ikwọta, dance round town, (ukwẹnta).

ikwulikwu, (I.A) powdered yam.

iḳwum, trap.

ilẹle ọkụ, flame.

ile nkọ, sharp tongue.

(di) îlê, strong.

ili n'asa (A), seventy.

ili n' asatọ (A), eighty.

ilinatẹgẹte, nineteen.

ili n' atọ (A), thirty.

ili n'ese (A), fifty.

ili n' eši (A), sixty.

ili tegete (A), ninety.

ílŏ, trouble, pain (mental), anger.

ílŏ, trunk (elephant).

îlŏ' outside.

ilogo, followers of orhene.

ilonye, helpless.

iluku, (As) big street.

ime, inside ; pregnancy ; pregnant.

imẹ ife, doing something.

imẹju, liver.

įmį mbwago, nose with wide nostrils.

imi mpia, hook nose, necrosed nose.

ímulĭmù, minute, tiny ; piece of a thing.

imăgọ', cunning.

inė, play, dance at ekwensu—

　　tata bu ine, uje, there is a play, (dance) to-day.

ìnů, story.

ìnů, bitter.

ìnů ìnů, bitter.

inyako, a girl's game.

įnya linya, broken things.

inyångà' proud.

inyari, millet.

inyeyọ, strainer (basket).

inyį (alo), heavy.

ínyí, dirty.

ìnyi (A), wood used by blacksmith; sasswood poison obtained
　　from same was in use for ordeals.

(ndi) inyom (=ndiom) [Abọ̇], women.

iraga (H), flower of corn.

įrånčà', everyone.

irhadi (IA), basket, sieve.

irhe, yam stock (fence).

ìrů, (A), slaves.

įrú, face,

įrù na azu, to and fro.

irurume, shaking.

išá', crayfish.

įså, rattle.

isagili, bullet.

isăka (Okp), rattle.

isanča (Abǫ), every people; all.

ise afia, cost price.

ísí, head, head of house, chief, sense, issue.

ȋsȋ (A), six.

ȋsi, smell.

isi, blind in both eyes.

ișia, crayfish.

iši alo, pollution.

ȋsẹfiẹ ụzǫ, other road, wrong road.

ísíkbẹ̀, edge, branch (palm).

isikei, (Og), hair in patch at back.

isikpoto (Ala), mark outside angle of eye.

isimwǫ (As., Ib.), woman on whose head eagle feather has been put.

isí ǫwa, ?conical head.

isisi, ǫka, corn cob.

isodi, going to live with husband.

isusu, evil, bad luck.

ịta, feather ordeal.

ítằ, proverb, story.

ita obǫ́, story to guitar accompaniment.

ịtali, whip, switch.

iteni (Ogw), nine.

ite osisi, stumps of trees (many).

iti bwili, thick (cloth).

ȋtị kịli (=ozu), palm wine from field tree.

(di) ịtịnkpu, wonderful.

itŏkwẹlẹgwe, workers (companies of young men).

itolito, weak.

itŏlo (Al.), pipe head.

itǫna, iron pot.

ituile, blister on tongue.

iwolo, cast skin.

ȋwŭ, seed.

ȋwŭ (As.), dance at New Year.

ȋwŭ, order, commandment, law.

ȋwŭ, disgust.

iyá, yes.

iyãbwa, two-ply thread.

(onye) iyãiyã (A), sick man.

iyắjĩ, Yoruba.

iyẹne, valley.

iyi, mat maker.

íyĩ, small stone (thief swallows one as ordeal).

íyĩ, waterside (small water), spring.

iyi, loss.

iyitọ, first course of house.

iyọ (Okp.), kind of basket.

iyọlọ, casting net.

iyọtabụ, chorus.

iz abu, tension drum.

izĕ, borer (for palm tree).

ízè, watcher.

izẹle, sneeze.

izẹlu, working before arrival of owner (slave or pawn).

izizi, brushing off dust.

ízú (—uka, 7 days ; nta, 4 days), week.

izú (A), meeting.


já, praise.

jắ, bright red.

ja ainya (O), point a gun.

já àjà, cry.

jắ, cut up, bite.

ja aja, (stomach) rumbles.

ja ja, cut up (tobacco or any leaf).

jagili nẹnẹwe, spy on.

jakajaka, (cut) small.

jaṅwu, wither.

je (akwa), wear.

je kwalalasŭ, go straight ahead.

je ṅko, step over person's legs.

je nranra, march side by side.

ǰe nšiše, walk quietly.

ǰe ǫku, go fishing.

ǰe ozi, serve, go message.

ǰe tẹ, go far.

ǰẹbẹ́, put clothes on another.

ǰẹ b̆u, denounce.

ǰẹ̀débe, stop walking.

ǰẹko ákwá, be about to cry.

ǰẹkwasi, go straight; go again.

ǰemie, travel inland; travel into Hinterland.

ǰẹruka, go a little further.

ǰǐ, take.

ǰí, yam.

ǰi ǫnụmụzirhe, first yam tied at entrance of *irhe.*

ǰi owuwu, boiled yam.

ǰi, be enemies—

    munye aji, we are enemies.

ǰǐ, fold.

ǰi ẹǰi, fold (cloth).

ǰi ainyasii, keep eyes open.

ǰi aka, hope.

ǰi azụ ẹjẹ, walk backwards.

ǰi eǰiǰi, dress.

ǰi nǰi, make, be black.

ǰi ǫfǫ, be innocent.

ǰi ụgwǫ . . . owe (money) for . . .

ǰibe, break (with thumb and first finger).

ǰibe (ǰi), cut in big pieces.

ǰibe ainya, blink eyes.

ǰiga ǰiga, trembling, dizzy.

ǰigomya, (road) branch.

ǰigoinye, bend.

ǰiǰa, cry.

ǰi kẹbe, try hard.

ǰikobạ[ma], (to) bend.

ǰi oko, yolk.

ǰi oku; ǰi oku (Al.), yam. sp.

888

jili ọsọ, rush, begin to run.

(onye) jọ njọ, ugly.

jọwainya, become worse.

jú, refuse—

    ajụgom, I refuse.

jụ ajụjụ, ask.

jụ asia, ask.

jụ arụ, "cleanse" body and set free chicken.

jụ' oyi, become cold.

jụ ozụ arụ, purify corpse.

jú, (1) be full; (2) satisfy.

    ojum, I am satisfied; ọju, he refuses.

ju' afọ, satisfy.

ju' ẹju, fill.

jụbu, kill fowl for purification.

jụčo ọnụ, ascertain from.

jụlụ, be calm.


ká, be bigger than, let, draw line, grow old, spoil.

kả, carve, give notice of day, fix, guess.

ka (before verb), would have, ought to have.

ka (before verb), not yet.

ka (O), let, when, that.

ka, what—

    ka, nke mu naii, what is your business with me.

ká, pass, surpass—

    ókả, he passes.

ká áká, be dry (kạka).

ká iikả, be old—

    ká iikả, be older.

ka (fruit), be full grown.

kả ose, divine.

kà ụbọsi, fix day.

kả uka, converse, backbite.

kačinte, obstinate.

kado aba, put staple (*see* yi aba).

kadǫ ainya, note, observe.
kàfie, guess wrong.
—kaka, here and there—
   dẹkaka, scrawl, write here and there.
(ime) kala, be far advanced in pregnancy.
kalama, cunning man.
kalụ, blame, speak ill of.
kalụ nkalụ, speak ill of.
kanite arụ, increase in stature.
(onye) kantẹ, obstinate person.
kapu akapu, cancel.
kásì, comfort.
kåsị, be pre-eminent.
katǫtǫ, cross out, cancel.
kb, *see also* b.
kbá, pare, move away with stick.
kbá, trade.
kbá, cause.
k bá, walk, bend.
kbá, be needful.
kbá, rub.
kbá aka, throw into bargain.
kbá ife akụ, get property.
kbá isi, plait hair.
kbá mma, strike matches.
kbača aka n'ainya, do I, bad in spite of danger.
kbača isi, take out rotten seed, yam (after sprouting).
kbačal' ainya, be careful.
kbàfú, soon—
   kbafu akbàmvo ẹje, I soon go.
kbainya, comb, bring in order.
kbakala kbakala, confusedly; noise made by rat in house.
kbaiyali, leave (living being).
kbako (ji), cut off head of yam.
kbani, stir up.
kbanye, dash.
kbe ekbẹlu, pray.

kbe ikbe, slander, report.

kƁǫ, burn.

kƁǫ' iku (Al.), abuse.

kƁǫ mwǫ, curse.

kƁǫ nni, be spoilt.

kƁǫwa, split.

kƁo, collect.

kƁo ndu, shave newborn child's hair.

kƁoa isi, cut hair.

kboča, scrape.

kƁokƁǫ ụnǫ, break down roof.

kƁale, roll (self) up.

kƁoli' amu, repress laugh.

kƁolie, put (mashed yams) in mouth.

kƁome, gather, grow big (trees).

kƁǫpo, be loose (screw).

kƁopue, bore hole.

kƁosip' ota, to loose bow (Ezi) *i.e.*, end a matter by reporting
    to Iyase.

okpǫfufu kƁu, sweat.

kƁu, cover.

kƁu ìsì, be blind.

kƁu n'äkwä', sit on eggs.

kbu obǔ, take over title.

kƁu ȯkṗú, wear hat.

kƁụƁu, kill.

kƁu, mate.

kbuči, cover.

kbuči, smooth.

kƁučie, go back.

kƁue, cover (whole body).

kƁue, open.

kƁùfú, soon.

kbuo ìsì, be blind.

ké, be dressed, strike fire.

kĕ̈, create, share, be ready.

kὲ̃, divide.

kẹ̈ ẹbo (town) be divided, separate quarters.

kẹ ẹbwo, divide farm work.

kẹ ẹke, divide, share, take turn about.

kẹ̈, betroth.

kẹ kọnata (ibu), lighten (a load).

kẹ nke, spy.

ke, ge, not.

   ife erikẹnne, ŋothing is bigger.

ké, dress.

ké' abwu, tie bonds.

ké ájà, tie bundle on wall (A).

ké ji, tie yams—

   inẹkẹ́ ji, are you tying yams.

ké' kebe, tie.

ké ẹkikẹ, decorate.

kẹča, become bright, clear up.

kẹkẹ nta, snake species (slender, black).

kẹli, quickly—

   ọbu oiya mwadu naṅwu kẹli, it is a disease that kills
     quickly.

kẹlefofo, mad.

kẹli, go to man to betroth one's daughter;

   give child (not one's own), in marriage (irregularly).

kẹli, spy.

kẹli, get share.

kẹlia, be dwarfish.

kẹlu, get share; prepare.

kẹmu, divide in small pieces.

kẹni ọdo, put up tail.

kẹnye ṅwunye, give betrothed.

kepu, tie in knot.

kepu, untie (?)

kẹra, divide equally.

kẹsa, scatter (to find game, etc.).

kẹta, get share.

kẹtolo, see.

kẹtu, cut down.

kẹwa, divide.

kẹwapu (ta), separate from.

kili ínė, look at spectacle ; big dance.

kitakita, at once.

kitaṅwa (On), now.

kla-kla-kla  .  .  . , call to fowl.

klu-klu-klu  .  .  . , call to fowl.

 kǫ́, scrape.

kọ, collect.

kǒ' a ọgọlọ, mix water with palm wine.

kọ ẹfẹle, be scarce.

kọ (?) ụkọ, be scarce.

kọ ukọ, scratch.

kǫ̈, plant, grow (corn).

kọ ani, explain, dig ground.

kọ isi, explain.

kọ aši, provide food, serve out yams (to wife).

kọ isi, share.

kǫ̈, hang up, spread to dry.

kọ akoa, be dry.

kọ akọ, dry clothes.

kǫ́nsi, poison.

ko ẹko n'ani, run along ground (plant).

ko onuma, be excited.

ko ofu, be excited.

kobei ikum, make fast hook (ṅgu).

kọča nkọča, speak ill of.

koča nkoča, touch (many things).

kodẹte, bring down, unhook.

kọdiṅwọ, as it is now.

kodo, entangle.

kọfi ẹkọfi, twist, coil.

kokọ (ẹze), chatter (teeth).

kokoali, embrace.

kokọba, fold up.

kokọli, strike together.

kokopute, collect (things).

kǫkowasi, hang on.
kǫ́kwa (Uk), bush fowl.
koli koli, very hungry.
kolo, respect.
kǫlǫ, finished.
kolu ije, prepare for journey.
kǫ̊m kǫ̊m, all finished.
kǫṅ kǫm, not at all.
konie, start.
konili, get ready.
konyụ, blow out.
konye n' obala, wind (cotton).
kopu, take snake from roof with stick.
kǫ́rúlu iru, say what p. is (to his disadvantage).
kǫrúlu owa, declare a bastard, say what p. is (to his dis-
    advantage).
kǫ̊rúlú iru, bend head, look down.
kǫsa, declare.
kosi, lodge.
kǫwa, explain.
kṗ (smack with lips), call to a goat.
kṗa, plait.
kṗa alǫ, take alǫ title.
kṗa ji n'irhe, tie yams in fence.
kṗa nkṗa, be narrow.
kṗabǫ, touch to attract attention.
kṗača aka n'ainya, take care.
kṗača aka n'ainya, do cunningly.
kṗača isi, cut (hair).
kṗačaľ ainya, take care.
kṗačapu ęze, show teeth.
kṗado, choke (seeds).
kṗado nkṗado, lean against, crowd.
kṗafie ǫinya, release a trap.
kṗafuè, stray.
kṗafundo, soon.
kṗagǫ, walk up.

kp̣aji, break.

kp̣akp̣a (O.O), cotton tree.

kp̣akala kp̣akala, bean sp.

kp̣akala kp̣akala, very rough.

kp̣akp̣a julaju, not heavy.

kp̣akọ, shrink.

kp̣akọba (nko), collect.

kp̣akọta, collect with difficulty.

kp̣ali (tu), stir.

kp̣ạlã̃kwukwu, pigeon.

kp̣ankp̣ạna (Ala), butterfly.

kp̣anya isi, dress hair.

kp̣ap̣ube afọ, expiation.

kp̣asẹbe ọko, make up fire.

kp̣ata aka, do thing that will cause one's death.

kp̣ata ofibo, buy oil.

kp̣ata okụ, cause palaver.

kp̣e, strip bark.

kp̣e, steer.

kp̣e mwaru, rub oil.

kp̣eƀu, choke (seeds, etc.), kill.

kp̣ečapu agƀubo, bark.

kp̣eče, peel (bananas).

kp̣egọsi, report to.

kp̣ẹle, backbite.

kp̣eli, be a reproach to.

kp̣ọ, big.

kp̣ọ, no.

kp̣ọ, pick (bean).

kp̣ọ afa, name.

kp̣ọ arụ ididili, shiver with fear.

kp̣ọ asi, hate.

kp̣ọ ifŭlu, blossom.

kp̣ọ iru, see first thing in morning, be first to salute.

kp̣ọ iyi, abuse, curse.

kp̣ọ izu, call meeting.

kp̣ọ okụ, call (at a distance).

sion. checkp

kpọ n' . . ., pierce.
kpọ ṅkpu, shout.
kpọ ṅkpukpọ, drive (peg), fasten (door).
kpọ ṅku, be dry.
kpọ n' obu, shrug shoulders.
kpọ ntu, jump.
kpọ ogẹde, beat ogede (drum).
kpọ oinya, set trap.
kpọ ọkụ, burn.
kpọ omimi, dive.
kpọ okpọfufu kpo, perspire.
kpọ ụkpọ, be dwarf.
kpọ ụbọ, play stringed instrument.
kpọ ụzụ, buzz, make noise.
kpo aja, make bricks, mud balls.
kpo igwe, make of iron.
kpoba, be making bricks.
kpọba, expose for sale.
kpọba ụkwụ, kick.
kpọbata, call in.
kpobwado, gather, collect.
kpọbe oinya (O.O), set trap.
kpọča, clean (by burning).
kpočapu, take clean away, clean off, jump out.
kpọdebe, call near.
kpọdo akpọdo, nail, peg.
kpọdụ, walk slowly (like sick man).
kpofiale, catch hold of.
kpọfie, call by wrong name.
kpofiẹpu (sun), be past the meridian.
kpoga, expose for sale.
kpọko, come together.
kpọko iru, see face to face.
kpokpọ, spoil house, harass.
kpọkpọ ṅgẹne, hop.
kpolie, cut grass.
kpolu ọsọ, rush off.

kpǫnaba, call home.

kpǫni, jump.

kpǫni, wake person.

kpǫnye ǫko, put fire.

kpoze, dig (with hoe).

kpu n' ǫnu, carry in mouth.

kpu ukpulu, trace ground plan (foot).

kpu uzu, be blacksmith.

kpu ìsì, become blind.

kpu ǫku, be hot.

kpu ufu, faint.

kpuči ainya, close eyes.

kpučibido, secure by shutting up.

kpučie, shut up.

kpučita, cover.

kpuda, draw down.

kpudębe (ani), near (land).

kpudo (?), cover (on ground).

kpudo (mwǫ), put mud to make mwǫ.

kpukpu ęnunǫ, unroof house.

kpukpu aka, motion for silence.

kpukpulukpu, firmness, stiffness.

kpukpuęlie, stagger.

kpulu, take (animal).

kpulu kpulu, very soft.

kpumi, draw in.

kpumulia amu, repress smile.

kpunita, draw up.

kpupu, uncover.

kpuputa, creep out.

kpuruka, move aside.

kpwębu, oppress.

kpwęli, (1) report ; (2) summons.

ku, . . .

    ǫkulu ṅwantinti, it was a narrow shave.

ku, knock, sound bell.

ku, plant.

ku̱ (aku̱), pluck leaves.

 e̱mu ku̱ (H), have fever.

ku̱ ṅsî, poison.

ku̱ u̱gwo̱ o̱lu, pay for work—

    ku̱ u̱gwo̱ onobwo (O,O), throw one cowry (annually) into the bush (hunter who has killed bush cat).

ku̱ ume ṅgwe̱le, breathe one's last ; breathe very little.

ku, blow (wind).

ku aka, clap hands.

ku aka n'eku, knock at the door.

ku erhi (O.O), cook food.

ku mili, carry water from vessel.

ku n' . . ., pierce.

ku n'aka, nurse.

ku njȩnje (Al.), travel.

ku n'obi, hold to breast.

ku ofu, be angry.

kû, call to dog.

ku̱a azu̱, fish.

ku̱a o̱kpo̱, knock head with fist, fight.

kuba, carry in.

kuba, call in, cause to enter—

    perf. e̱kolŭmba, I carry in.

    okwoliya banu̱no̱, he calls him in.

kube̱, cease breathing.

kube e̱kube, die, pass away, blow over.

kube̱pu, be at point of death.

kuči, cover (with pot).

kučie, return wife to husband.

kuda, drop down.

ku̱do aka, fold arms.

kue̱li (trs.), stir.

ku̱ja, startle.

ku̱ko̱ e̱zé, chatter (teeth) (also on purpose).

kugide, hammer.

kuko̱ba, collect.

kukuba (aka), fold.

kule (ozu), wrap up body.

kŭlŭ kulu, soft, rotten.

kunye, hand over person to another.

kunyẹli, dip cup and drink, (palm wine).

kupute, (1) hand over someone to other man ; (2) take sick
    person to other place.

kusọ, start, jump.

kutọ, abuse, run down.

kutu, uproot.

kuwa, be famous.

–kwa, about to—
    ada kwạ n'ụzọ, he was about to fall by the way.

–kwa, not—
    atukwa n'uče, don't hesitate.
    ákokwa, don't plant.

kwǎ', aim.

kwá', prepare.

kwa ǎkwa', prepare nest (for egg).

kwa', remove (trans.).

kwa abwa, dislocate jaw.

kwa ani (ife), carry loads to other town on leaving.

kwa alili, lament.

kwa ẹlẹle, cry with grief.

kwa ife, sew up.

kwa ilolo nabọ, be in two minds.

kwa ṅkwukwuši, seize for debt or crime (only property).

kwa nši, have cough.

kwa ọčo, compensate for murder.

kwa okwala, cough—
    akwam odauṅ, I cough.

kwa ọnụ, make excuse.

kwa ošẹle, cry very angrily, refuse to obey.

kwa ošili, make very narrow road

kwǎ ṅwunye, take wife of another.

kwǎ ůtǎ', regret.

kwǎ' aka, push, urge.

(ji) kwa (intrs.), grow (yams).

kwá kwằ (H.), bush fowl.

kwaba ota, bend bow.

kwača akwača, peel.

kwača ji, peel.

kwači ǫčo, compensate for murder.

kwačie, take over house of dead man.

kwaye, push open.

kwainya, push in.

kwainya n' aka, die in person's hand.

kwaiye, push open.

kwakpǫ ainya, cry bitterly.

kwakǫba, gather.

kwakǫdo, sew together.

kwalằ, remove all.

kwali, bring out.

kwali, peel cooked fruit and eat.

kwanằ, become accustomed to—
    orhi akwanằgoa n' arụ, he is accustomed to steal.

kwapu ife (n'ụbwǫ), unload a boat.

kwatu, push down.

kwaye (ụzǫ), clear road.

kwę nto (i), say "yes."

kwe n'aka, shake hands.

kwe ṅkwa, promise.

kwe ụgwǫ, pay debt.

kwé' ota, string bow.

kwegǫsi, plead case.

kwęli ṅkwa, make promise.

kweni isi, nod.

kwérừbe, shake.

kwęzi ota, restring.

–kwǫ, (suffix of interrogation).

kwǫ mili, bale.

kwǫ', grind.

kwǫ́, ride.

kwǫwusa, ladle water on.

kwo ękwo, pull up (plant).

kwojili, rush.

kwo ṅwunye, take wife (without service).

kwó, singe (fowl).

kwŏ̃ ekwolo, be envious.

kwŏ̃ ọṅwu, be at death's door.

kwọba, bend.

kwọba ọkwŭkwọ, stick and bend a fish.

kwọča aka, rub hands.

kwoče̩, (1) pluck (fowl); (2) pull out fine hairs.

kwolu ibu, be ready for load.

kwopu, be loose (tooth).

kwopu, take out tooth.

kwọri, shrug.

kwosi (wa) afia n'u̩zọ, stop on road to market.

kwọte, wake person.

kwọwa, divide (farm).

kwu̩', pay.

kwu̩ ṅgọ, pay bride price—
    àkwŭm ọ̊nồ̊å, I pay price.
    e̩kwŭm ọ̊nồ̊å, I talk about price.

kwú̩ akwu̩, be beautiful.

kwu̩' alu̩lů̩, be misty.

iwu, kwu, turn away from, be disgusted with—
    nni e̩kwugom iwu, food disgusts me.
    iwue e̩kwugom, he disgusts me.

kwu, sharpen (first time).

kwú, stand, suffocate.

kwu, speak—
    òkwŭlŭ, he said.

kwu ifulif' oku, rave.

kwu iyi, swear.

kwu muli muli, whisper.

kwu ofe̩ge, tell lie.

kwu obwalala, stand straight.

kwu ọnu̩, fix price.

kwu ọta, march round town at burial.

kwu̩ba, place.

kwu̱ḅu, hang.

kwube oḳu, be talking.

kwubi afa, run down some one.

kwuḅu, hang person.

kwuča, stand a little apart.

kwu̱da̱, (water) run down.

kwu̱da akwu̱da, take down (whole of a thing).

kwudẹbe, stop speaking.

kwudẹbe oḳu, stop talking.

kwudide, go on speaking.

kwudo, meet, arrive in time.

kwudomba (aǰa), be near.

kwu̱fe, hang.

kwufẹlie, stand behind (in searching) and not go in.

kwufie (ọnu̱), pronounce wrong.

kwu̱gba, hang (on peg).

kwugide, stand still.

kwukṗa ọnu̱, talk in lower voice.

kwu̱kwọ, rub hands.

kwu̱kwọ (mma), sharpen (on another).

kwu̱lie, stay long.

kwùlǒʼ kwulo, shout to drive off cow.

kwu̱lu̱, stop (person).

kwùlù, very many.

kwulu ẹfẹ (m), be independent.

kwulu nšanša, stop opposite (canoe, person).

kwuni, wake up.

kwuniri mwáinyẹ̈, rebel.

kwu̱pu̱, take off, have vent.

kwusa, proclaim.

kwusaba, publish.

kwuwe, explain.


lá, cohabit, drink, sleep—

  ȯlá, he drinks ; ȯlá, he copulates.

la iyi, swear.

lă, entice.

lă ǫnu, ascertain from.

lådo, coax, retain by coaxing.

lainye, entice into.

laǰu, drink to the full.

lakwaba, (1) hush child to sleep; (2) console.

lålǎ, deceive.

lali, drink some.

lalu, drink part.

lama lama, shining.

lamulia, smile.

lapu, drink all.

laru alaru, coagulate, " sleep."

låta, attract, coax.

lé, sell, burn, rot.

le ife obube, sell retail.

le n'ębwę, sell wholesale.

le nnu aiyaka, sell salt in powder.

lę nnu ǫkṗokṗo, sell salt retail (in "cups").

le nto ǫmuma, buy powder retail (in measure).

lebwusia, consume with fire.

lęča nlęča, be impertinent.

lędę, (wick) burn away, be burnt.

lęgelęge, child.

leni, (Uk.) rotten.

(di) lęte, (O.A) level.

lí, climb.

li' (ęlięm, a.), become less.

lí afa, take title name.

li antitia, be disabled (?).

lí aru ęfe, be at ease, free.

li atu, embezzle.

lí ísí (Uk.), be free.

lí iyi, take oath.

lí ǰu afǫ, be satiated.

lí ali ani, creep.

lí mpęli, miscarry; "miss fire" (bow).

lí n' èkû, boast after eating.

lí ṅgo, take bribe.

lí ṅgọ, take bride price.

lí nra, fine.

li…nra, take object as fine from defaulting person or town.

lí (ife) ntogwa, eat all sorts of things.

lí nzẹle, take dignity.

lí ọkwằ' (or 2-3), misfire.

lí olili, have feast.

lí olili ọč̆o, destroy property of murderer.

lí onini, make peace.

lí oruru ose, eat forbidden thing.

lǐ, be good (medicine).

—lia, each other.

   jutalia nụ, ask each other questions.

liằ', grind corn a second time.

lǐằ', slice.

liå, hello.

liạ̊, be sick.

liača osisi, smooth tree (with ? adze).

libe mwadu ụkwụ, walk on someone's heels.

libido, be hemmed in.

liči ọno, (1) eat something that disagrees ; (2) be sensible.

lịdata, descend.

lịfẹge, pass over.

lịfeta, climb over.

lifọ, eat part.

ligb̃u, defraud.

lịgolu alịgolu, climb.

liju, eat enough.

likẹbe, eat enough.

likọ, eat together.

likọ elikọ, eat together.

likp̃u, overwhelm.

lịkwasi, climb up, upon.

likwo, (tooth) be loose.

likwue, eat all.

lịla, make stupid.

lịla (ṅkbu), cry.

lịla nlịla, act stupidly.

lipụ, eat all.

lita, inherit, eat from.

lita n' ẹlẹle, gain.

lita n' uku, inherit.

lite, (canoe) carry.

lọ́, contradict, put small stick, spoil, work.

ló, hurt.

lọ̣, rub with oil.

lọ́, sacrifice, dream.

lö, think.

ló Agu, (A) put peg for Ago.

lọ́ mwọ, sacrifice to mwọ.

lọ́', twist (fibre).

ainyaṅwu lọ́, the sun bends, *i.e.*, (it is) afternoon, 4.0 or
5.0 p.m.

lụ̈ (alọ), become thick.

lọ...ainya, accustom...to house; give medicine to; (1) keep
goat at home; (2) make madman's eyes " cool."

lọ̣ mwanu, rub oil.

lọ́', cut.

lọ́ afifia, weed.

lọ́, work, build.

lọ́, be faulty.

lọ́ alọ, be defiled.

lọ ụnọ, build house.

lọ́' ubwo, make farm.

lọ́ ụka, have dispute.

lọ̈ ụkwụ, limp.

lọ' nsọ, do forbidden thing.

lọ̣, stick in.

lö, point out.

lö aka, point out.

lö osisi, plant stick.

lo ilo, hurt.

lo oka, deny, object.

lŏ (arụ), be tired.

arụ lŏ, be tired.

lŏ, think—

ẹlom, I think.

ẹloẹm, I thought.

lo ẹlo, think.

lobakwasi, begin to work again.

loᵬu (I.A.), choke.

lọfiẹpu, shoot (arrow), pull trigger.

lọkọ, hush.

lọ̀kṕọ́, loiter.

lonata, think about, consider.

lopu ife, stop thinking of something.

lọrube, walk round.

lọta, (1) clean farm; (2) get.

lọta ife, gain—

ilọta ife, gain by working.

ílŏtå ife, remember.

lota ife, remember—

ẹlotẹm, I remember.

lụ ẹgẹnẹgẹ, stand on tip toe.

lụ ịru, pretend anger.

lụ nzu, rub chalk.

lụ ụzọ iyi, clean channel.

lú' ainya, notice.

lú' aka, reach.

lú' ṁbå' (lú ṁbå?), reach full size.

lú' ógŏ, reach full age.

lú' ani, settle.

lú' arụrụ, breed worms.

lu ẹlu, rot (wood).

lu ẹlu, (yams) grow.

lu ẹli, (hawk) circle.

lú' inyi, be dirty.

lu ịzizi, tickle; be on edge (teeth).

lu ẹzé ịzizi, be on edge (after eating sweet things) [causes teeth to chatter, as if cold].

lú' izi, be on edge.

lú' mili, wade.

lu okṗukṗa, (nuts) be rotten.

lụ čiọlụ, do other's work—

     ilụ či ọlụ onye, whose work are you doing.

lụlụ nlụlụ, do evil (stupid man).

lụsi (ọlụ), finish (work).

lube, rise (river).

lube, reach.

lǔe, (yams) be overcooked.

luj̆ue, (moon), be full.

luo mili (As), shake down water.


maču ite, put fire in pot, so that it is good for water.

m̃bá̰, town (people and land).

m̃bá̰, tree species, *Holaripena wulfsbergii.*

m̃bǎ', no.

m̃bá, head of corn.

m̃bá, rebuke.

(da)m̃bǎ', starvation.

m̃bá̊dá̊, slope.

mbafọ, side.

mbakata mbakata, walk of stout person with fat legs.

m̃bá̊lá̊ ataba, tobacco leaf (European).

mbaligwe, sky.

mbalọtọ, naked messengers of Benin.

mbalukb̃o (O. O), seat in verandah.

mbana, (Obuluku) farm road.

mbanna (Og.), sept ; the same as umunna.

m̃bė̃, tortoise.

m̃bě̃, pledge.

m̃bẹ̰, rat.

m̃bė̃, calabash (salt).

mbẹbẹl' ainya, eyelashes.

mbelẹ́ju ukpe, broken pot (used as lamp).
mbi, bird species.
mbia, hiding.
ḿbia, lesser guinea fowl (thick bush).
mbia, travelling.
mbiambia, stranger.
mbịdịmbwe, fish species.
mbili, small child.
mbịli, slave.
ḿbọ̀, swamp in which *Raphia* grows.
ḿbọ̀ (O), baby (female) (till mother conceives again).
ḿbọ̀, vengeance.
ḿbọ̀ (utulu), red yam sp.
m̀bọ̀, one.
m̀bọ́, ground squirrel.
m̀bọ̀ (A), two.
m̀bọ̀, nail.
m̀bòbå, hiding.
mbwala, thin.
m̀bwala, line.
ḿbwålå, tension drum.
mbwalaku, isamisi, small pox.
mbwalaṅko, dry wood, faggot.
mbwạma, float.
m̀bòbå, brush (for sand on seed yam).
ḿbõbọ̀, retracting oath, magic (alose).
m̀bòbọ, half.
mbobwa, part of irhe; stick of yams.
mbobwo ọkoko, perch (fowl).
mboẹke (O. O), red yam.
m̀bõlå, frog.
mbolimi, giddiness.
m̀bòlò, missile.
mbụ azụ, dried fish.
mbul' isi, (portion for) each.
mbubu, mark on tree, step.
mbubu (A), mark on chest, belly.

mbulu, going to meet.

mbulugudu, valley.

mbuṅwute, portable.

mbwa (H), "friend."

mbwả', sherd.

mbwả', pot rest.

mbwá (A), wrestling, struggle.

mbwàdà, downhill.

mbwàdả, ṅw' ilọta, juiker.

mbwafụfụ (I.A., Ubul), eaves—

   mili mbwafụfụ, water from the roof.

mbwagoni, uphill.

mbwáɤ̊lỉ, being no better (sickness).

mbwákà, ring—

   ẹ́ṅwẻlủmụ̀ mbwảkả, I have a ring.

mbwakwa, support (mud) for pot.

mbwani, first course of house.

mbwani, turning pestle in pounding yams.

mbwani, stumbling.

mbwalụnọ (Ub.), room.

(otẹke) mbwẻ, half a bushel.

mbwẹde (O. O), a red yam.

mbwẹku, miscarriage (animal).

mbwẹle, lease rods.

mbwẹmbwẹ, low.

mbwidi, (Ob), a hollow under the ukbo.

mbwọ̀, shutter.

mbwỏ, board (to carry mud).

mbwọtọ (Al.), unplanted portion of farm.

mẹ, become.

mẹ ìsì (H), become blind.

mẹ, overcome, conquer, injure, affect—

   ume ṅwa nẹmea, all his children die.

mẹ, (smoke) suffocate.

mẹ agadi, be old.

mẹ ainya agagaga, dazzle.

mẹ akaǰe, make jealous, mock.

me . . . akusǫ, cause to jump, startle.
me amala, be gracious.
me ainya ǫgaga, see indistinctly.
me azani, disgust.
me ǫbubǫ, respect.
me ǫmǫm ife, complete title.
m(ǝ́) ǫnu m' ani, try all you can.
me if' ozo, take ozo title.
me lama lama, shine.
me mpo, act like madman.
me n'ike, do violently.
me ǫgǫ, do kindness.
me soe ife nagua, do as one pleases.
me so ife n'obie, do as one pleases.
me ṅkwa, make agreement; make promise.
me ok̇enya, be mature (40 years).
me omume, act.
me onyinye, give present.
ṁǫ̌ (A) or mmě, red (blood).
me arụ agusǫ, tremble.
me ṅwaboa (woman), reach puberty.
me nyoi, say no more.
mǫ̌ pulu pulu, be very soft.
mǫbǫ ikṗo, make heap.
mǫbi (ǫiyi), cause to quarrel.
mǫči, do again.
mǫči nti, be disobedient.
mǫdide, do against.
mǫfie, do wrong.
mǫfǫ ǫmǫmife, leave title unfinished
mǫgwali, requite.
mǫyali, move round.
mǫju, fill.
mǫjua ainya, tame (animal).
mǫkǫ (A), copulate.
mǫkwụlo, take vengeance
mǫli, take water.

mẹni, stir up.

mẹnya ụkwụ, walk slowly.

mẹpụ, undo.

mẹri udu (H), be silent.

mẹso, deal with.

mẹte, rouse.

mẹtọ, spoil, defile, soil.

mfẹde, crossing.

mfẹne, unknown—

   ádìmu mfẹ̀nẹ̀, am I unknown.

   ádímù mfẹ̀nẹ̀, I am unknown.

mfiče olulu, roller for cotton.

mfiẹle, noose in obwẹbwe.

mfó, ant (nest in tree).

mí mmwa, draw sword.

mị anụ (azụ), dry, smoke meat (fish).

mị ọko, smoke pipe.

mị ẹmị, be deep, skilled, mysterious.

mị mmịmị, suck.

mi, go slowly.

mikpọ akwa, burst out crying.

mili arụ, moisture, oil secretion of skin—

   oṅwẹrọ mili arụ, he has a dry skin.

mili li (ya), be drowned.

mili ọbobo, drizzle.

mili olulu, rising.

mịpua, walk slowly.

mịpụta, take out, suck out.

mmangọ, cooking knife.

mmẹ̃, red (blood).

mmù, gum (from tree).

mmwafia, bruise.

mmwàfià, blister (broken).

mó', cut big wound with matchet.

mŏ, cry.

moani, buzzer (toy); bull roarer (used at night, dry season)

mòtò mòtò, flourishing.

ṁpả lụzọ, narrow.

mpala, step.

mpata (I.A.), circular box of iroko.

ṁpé, widow's cloth.

mpẹ̌ji, small seed yam (Al.).

ṁpỉ, horn.

ṁpiá, hunter's path.

mpío, small hole, path.

ṁpĭpí, top of tree.

ṁpịpị, cut goat.

mpipi ani, spit of land, sand.

ṁpọ̣, fish sp.

mpọkọ, bamboo pole.

mpọlo (Al.), working-cloth (dress).

ṁpọ̣m, robber.

ṁpụ́, for nothing.

mụ́ amụ́, bear child.

mụ (ukp̣e), light (lamp).

mụ̃, shine.

mụ̃, I—

    mụ na isim, I myself.

mụ̃˜ amụ, learn.

mu ụnọ, be tame.

mụ́˜, sharpen.

mụ̀ mbọ, pinch.

muba ije, learn to walk.

muke muke (Uk.), hunter.

mụli, growl—

    amulim, I growl.

    amuliem, I growled.

mụṅwu mụde, sharpen well.

mụnye, learn more.

munye, we (he and I).

mụpụ amụpụ, laugh aloud.

mụpụta, learn thoroughly.

muru (da), swoop down on.

mụ́sỉ mụ̃sỉ, shining (with oil).

mwa', beat (rain).

mwá', know.

mwa', make hole with stick.

mwá, be ignorant of, jump, know, shake, sound, forbid.

mwå, plant, knot, smell, go faster, suck in air.

mwá ainya afia, be clever trader.

mwá' aka, be friendly, tame.

mwá aka, slap.

mwa' ụla, slap.

mwá' akpåla, thunder.

mwá àkwà, make bed, build bridge.

mwá akwukwọ, put out leaves.

mwá ámụmå, prophesy.

mwa' mwọ, prophesy, imprecate.

mwá åmùmå, lighten (?).

mwá (amwa), make hole with stick in ground.

mwá arụ nni, tremble.

mwá ašiši anụ, imitate animal's call.

mwá' ẹbu, get mouldy.

mwá ẹbubu, mark.

mwá ẹkwe, beat drum, proclaim.

mwa eyu, become mouldy.

mwá ife, have sense.

mwá ifulu, blossom.

mwá ikp̌e, condemn.

mwá ịta, try ita ordeal.

mwá iwu, make law, proclaim.

mwá ji, stick yams.

mwá mbulu, throw sticks.

mwá mili, put water on sick person.

mwá mmá, be beautiful.

mwa nbibi aka, push chest or throat.

mwá (nnono), throw stick (at bird).

mwá ọgọ, be grateful, courteous.

mwá ọ́kwà, announce.

mwá osisi, plant cutting, stick.

mwa' ọso, suck teeth (disgust).

mwa' ube, stab (with spear).

mwá' ummà, pierce with sword.

mwá ụnọ, level floor.

mwằ, measure.

mwằ ụnọ, measure house.

mwằ abuba, be fat.

mwằ isi, smell.

mwằ isisị, sniff, scent (as dog).

mwẚ, weigh (corn).

ṃwằ', but, if, whether.

mwa anụ, smoke animal out.

mwa imwằ, be proud, be overbearing—

mu k'inama imwa, is it to me that you are insolent.

mwa ji, cut (yam) in big pieces.

mwa nzuzu, rub dry leaves.

mwa ọnụ, abuse big man, talk improperly, talk with one's superior (e.g., small boy and old man).

mwaba (sia) (Al) afọ, lie belly to ground.

mwabali, catch hold of.

mwabwari, catch hold of.

mwača (ọnụ), rinse (mouth).

mwačasili, know well.

mwači, come into leaf.

mwači, fill hole (in floor, canoe).

mwačie, throw back.

mwadu (mwa ndu, person living), person.

mwadu ka iba mwa, marks on upper lip.

mwafe, jump over.

mwafiale, catch hold of.

mwafiali, embrace, hold tight.

mwafue, splash over.

mwayali, jump about.

mwainya ọgọlọ, palm wine from raphia.

mwáinyè, fighting.

mwaji, jump and break (As.).

di mwaji, doubled.

mwaji, fold (once).

mwaka ifi, for the sake of.

mwaka, be unable—

mmwaka ṅkẹwọ, I cannot that; I could not guess it.

mwaka ya, therefore.

mwakoa, knock together.

mwakpọ, know well.

mwali, shake.

(ani) mwali arụ (of place), suit (person)—

ọlụ amwalego arụ, be accustomed to work.

mwalu aṭo, mention—

amwalum aṭo ẹfụ mwadụ, I mention seeing a man.

mwamu nni, shiver—

arụ amwa mu nni, I shivered with fear, cold.

mwáni, eleven (also H).

mwani, jump up.

mwaṅwụ, recognize.

mwapiá, running loop (A.O.).

mwạrọ, annual sacrifice to ancestors.

mwarube, shake (liquid).

mwa si, be all right—

enu ga mwasi lii, the world will be all right for you.

mwasi arụ, suit.

mwati (onu), lengthen (neck).

mwatu, throw stones (at fruit).

mwatu, knock down.

mwawu, become " high " (meat, fish).

mwawụ ọko, put coal in pipe; draw at pipe (to light it).

mwazido, put down load unhelped.

mwe ọji, (Okp.) pay bride price.

(onye) mwọ̃, lazy man, idiot, fool.


ná, guard, etc.

ná, take.

ná atune, examine.

ná efone, examine.

ná ẹloga, walk listlessly.

ná liali n'ani, creep on ground.
ná n'iyi, perish.
ná oli, sink.
ná otó, collect tribute.
nǎ, seize.
ǹà' niggardly.
na mbobwǫna (anklet edge), ankle high.
na ǹgiga, over the fire.
nabi, two.
nabǫ abǫ, two coloured.
nači, close (hole), with pot.
ną̀i íyî, take oath.
ną̀i íyi, perish.
nainye, hand.
nąiyąiya, change.
nakǫ, about to go home.
nakǫ anakǫ, go home.
nakpojiji arụ, terrible.
nakwa (bẹ di), go (finally) to reside with husband.
nąkwẹ, dancer.
nakwe, dance.
nakwu, go to—
    ani anakute, the town goes to collect a fine (As).
nali ẹze, usurp.
nali ibu, take load from, some one.
nanari, escape from.
nani ife, take something away.
naniyi, vain, useless.
onye nanu unu, hustler.
narå, interrupt.
nata (onye) ǫfumma, receive well.
ǹboǹbo (At.), side of road.
ńčå, soap.
nčąnča, not at all.
nčaǹwu, dry season.
(onye) nče, sentry.
nči, *mungos caffer*, mungoose.

nči kwệle kwệle, rubber.
nčinči, corner.
ndaba, overclouding (moon or sun).
ndabudu, valley, abyss.
ndẹdogŭle, stupid.
ndẹji mili, rumbling of rain.
ndẹkubwẹne, stupid.
ndệlẹ̆ (A!.), size.
ndičie, (I. A, Uk.), men who have not taken ọkpala title.
ndičie (O.O), men who have taken orhai title.
ńdỏ (ičẹndo), substitute.
ńdỏ (A), pigeon.
ńdỏ', life.
ǹdỡ, expression of sympathy.
ndodo, skewer for yams—
    ndodo adẹji tabwaka, a skewer does not come out empty.
ňdodo, root growing out of earth.
ndokƀu, last course on wall.
ndokwe, peace.
ndoru, changeable.
ǹdữ, conductor—
    abum onye ndŭi, I am your leader.
    ndu ụgwọ, take creditor to own debtor and transfer debt.
    akƀam ndu, I come back from escort.
ǹdú, hair of baby.
ǹdủ, boil (rat or fowl).
ǹdữ ákƀånî, handle of shield.
ndu n'ume, thing that lives.
ndúdu ílèm—
    inadúm ndudu îlẻ, you are asking me things I do not
    know.
nduju, man who has children.
ne, not—
    ǹke bụ ụmụa sole, ǹke nẹbụlụ umua, siẹnu, those
    that are her children follow her, those that are not, go up.
    či ẹ̌jine, when the day is not done, before the day is
    over.

nẹ́, look, etc.

ne, sign of habitual—

    ubwọ nuwa nelu ibu, this canoe carries a load.

nẹ́ azani, despise.

nẹ́ onine, observe.

ne (O.O), have.

né ọlụ, entertain workers.

né' obiama, entertain stranger.

onye nẹbẹ n'okụ, one who comes to the point slowly.

n'ekatọ obite, immediately.

onye nẹkḃe ịta (O.O), speaker of proverbs.

n'ekpe omẹsi, afterwards.

onye nẹku okḃolikọ ọnụ, loud talker (gruff voice).

onye nẹku tạinyu tạinyu, one who talks in squeaky, high

    voice (like white woman).

nẹtẹ, visit.

nezi ainya, beware.

ni (Al.), go past ?

ni (O.O), go and seek.

ni', still.

nǐ, bury.

nibe, hide (money).

n'ibijọ, at once.

n'ibilizọ, suddenly.

n'igilizọ, suddenly.

nili, be lying down (child or old person).

ṅjá', brass rings for legs.

njakakḃa, forked, jointed, six toed.

njakolo, stomach ache ; ?worms.

njeaka, wrist.

nji oifiá, bush round alose in farm.

njojo olulu, stick on which cotton is held for spinning.

ṅlọ̀gọ̀, bent.

nne nzu, nne ọzuzu, suckling mother.

nne ọmumu, prolific mother.

nni åkọ̀, corn paste.

nni ba ọla (pronounced bu'ọla), old food.

nni ẹfifie, midday meal.

nni ụnọṅwu, food provided by suitor of widow.

nnini, stubborn.

ńnǒnǒ, bird—

  nnono kwụlo, edege (O), nnono ebwa ẹtakwụlu (A), many birds are sitting.

nnu odẹne, sugar.

nnu ọrira, powdered salt.

nọ (Uk), consider.

nọ́ (nụ́), hear, be hot.

nọ̀, live, stay.

nọ́, spread, sit, be under someone.

nọ anọ, live apart (menstruous woman).

nọ́ n' une, (H), observe.

nọ̀ ọdo, tarry.

n' ọ̃bazu, (a) in (his) absence

nọbido, come near.

nọ bido, stop (person).

nụ̆ča ite, light leaves in pot.

nọčada isi, brush hair.

nọči ụnọ, take charge of house.

nọdo naṅkiti, sit down in idleness.

nọdu, sit.

  nọdula n' une, beware of him (sit for him and look).

nọgọ bạ[ma] (trs.), bend.

nọkọba, sit together.

n'ọkọlọkọlọ, around.

nọkwe, stay longer.

nọrube, surround.

nọruka, stay long, sit on one side.

nọso, sit beside.

nọw' ẹse, (Uk), quarrel.

nọzie, sit straight.

ṅrǎ, fine.

ṅrǎ', (O), comb.

nrạinya, equal.

ṅráká, handful.

ṅrá̯kǎ, equal.

nranr' u̯bọsi, midday.

nrire, slow.

nru mwọ, iru mwọ, offerings for mwọ (suitor's).

nruru, greediness.

nsála, pepper soup, soup without oil, thin.

nsapo, village dying out.

ṅsí, dung, fæces.

ṅsî, poison.

nsiǎma, note, reminder.

nsigŏ̯lu, not straight, zig-zag.

nsikḃo, (O.O), rod used in the loom.

nši̯kọ, crab.

nsi̯kọ, back of knee.

nsikṗu, putting hammer to half cock.

nso, (O.O), loom post.

ṅsȯ, following after.

ṅsȯ (O), short.

nsọk ṗulu, respect for.

nsọkwu, nonsense, foolish thing.

    ime ife nsọkwu, to do a foolish thing.

nsu n' isi, head kerchief.

ṅtǎ', hunting.

ṅtǎ, small.

ntako, thing left over water level by subsidence.

ntala, lines of a house on ground.

ntá ṟu̯ṟu̯, ant (black nest in tree).

nte, long (life, etc.).

n̯ti̯, cheek.

ntiḃwo, wrinkles.

ntili = ntala.

(onye) nti nkṗo, deaf.

ntite, far.

ntiti, beater (for cloth).

ṅtȯ, (A), toll.

ṅtȯ, ashes.

ṅtọ̇, kidnapping.

ntọ́' ebwẹ, (O), gunpowder.

ǹtobwǎnto, very stout.

ntọke, coral bead.

ǐtòkò, (O. O), patch of hair on right of head.

(di) ntǒlo, difficult.

ǹtọ̀tọ̀, (O), tally—

ẹwẹlum ntọ̀tọ̀ ẹgò, I take a tally, i.e., one for each ten.

ǹtọ̀tọ̀, long ribs (of house).

ntoto mili, dripping (from trees or house).

ǹtụ́, sting, sore.

ǹtụ́, guile.

ǹtú, small house, e.g., for forge.

ǹtǎ, nail.

ntukpọ, impertinent.

nụ́, boil.

nụ́, burn (pot).

nú, buy palm wine.

nụ̀ǐ⁻, fight.

nụ́, marry.

nụ anụ, (fufu) be viscous.

rụ́ isì, smell.

(nọ) nụ ǹwunye, marry wife—

nụ́ okụ, obey.

nụ́' ọrira, hear sound.

nụ nǰi, make black—

anum nǰi, I am black after working in the sun and washing (goes off in one day).

nụ ono, walk quickly.

nú', push.

nǔ inu, give riddle; be bitter.

nụba nǰi, turn black.

nuǐi, close.

nuǐiẹte, push back.

nụfie, hear wrong.

nufu, mislead.

nukpo (trs.), sink.

núkǔ, big.

nunu, entangle, be entangled.

(onye) nunu nunu, (A) clumsy, careless.

nupu, push off, leave harbour.

nupu isi, rebel.

nụta, get by fighting.

nutu, push down.

nyá, stick.

nyá (nti), listen.

nya, at the same time.

nya, be close to.

nya, bask.

aro (ai) nya, be tried.

nya ọnụ, deny before alose.

nya ụbwọ, paddle.

nyaba, roast corn.

nyača, wash out.

nyačapu, fade (colour).

nyači, close (wound).

nyadata, pull down to water (branch).

nyado, stick, adhere.

nyado (aka), lay (hand) on.

nyafu, yesterday.

nyagali, be proud.

nyagọba, bend.

nyaji, break.

nyakudo, cling to.

nyali, tie round neck (as bag).

nyali nyali, luke warm.

nyapelu, break off a bit.

nyapu (abwa), take off (jaw).

nyata ụbwọ, bring to land (canoe).

nyatu, break off (something growing or standing in ground) break down.

nyawa break (something soft).

nyẹ́ ala, suckle child.

nyẹ kwo [caused by abwa], dark patch in skin, wrinkles.

nyẹ́ ṅkwa, make promise.

nyẹ nzu, pronounce judgment for.

nyẹ olo, pronounce judgment for.

nyẹ ụbwọ, land canoe.

nye, call name.

nyeče (Okp.), shave half (widow).

nyị̃ alọ, be heavy ; be too much for—
    enye nyị mwado, mwọ ara, if the decision is too much
    for men the mwọ decide.

nyị̃, weighty.

nyi˘, pass, climb, step over.

nyịbu, load to death.

nyịdo, load heavily.

nyiyẹ, foolish thing.

nyụ̃, peep.

nyụ̀, quench; go out, pour out.

nyụ̀ århôlô, break wind.

nyụ̆ča, examine.

nyụkụba ainya, close eyes.

nyụsa, break wind all about.

nza, fly whisk (short).

ñ̃zá, bird (small, eats ọdodo seed).

ṅzå, casting lots.

ṅzá' (O), support.

ṅzå', brush for yam (of palm leaves).

ṅzå', flower of corn.

ṅzå', cow's tail.

ṅzå', strainer.

ṅzå' ọkọči, middle of dry season.

nzi, (A.l.) messenger.

nzizi odọ, inner bark used for cord, etc.

nzo (? H.), rubber.

ṅzọ̀', favourite wife.

nzọpu (O. O), pit-trap.

nzozo, ground leaf.

ṅzû, common sense.

ṅzụ̆ únọ̀, house (full sized).

nzụlili, (I.A.), mark under eye.

ńzůtẹ́, stolen object.
ńzůtě, meeting.
nzuzu, foolish thing.
ńaču, half broil.
ńgá, there! take it!
ńgå, loop holding up trap (ibudu).
ńgạ̀', iron bar, gag, prison.
ńgada ńga ẹfifie, 12.0–1.0 p.m.
ńgágó, shuttle.
ńgalaǰiǰi, trembling.
ńgaliga, contemptible.
ńgắnå, fork (of legs), branch.
ńgana, perverse.
ńgazowo ẹ̀bî, fish species.
ńgwẹku, name of Okpala title at Oniča Olona.
ńgẹ ńgẹ', one by one.
ńgî̧, thou.
ńgi̧ga, fish spear.
ńgiga, place where basket (nkpọdo) is tied.
ńgi̧li afọ uku (nta), bowel.
ńgo, lye.
ńgọ̀', bride price.
ńgò, wonderful.
ńgò', trial, test.
ńgò', bribe.
ńgońgo, side of road.
ńgů, crook, hook for fruit.
ńgů, tree.
ńgu ilo, pleurisy.
ńguainya, wife beater.
ńgůgů, 780 or 800 cowries.
ńgůgů (O), bundle.
ńgugwọ unọ, corner of roof (inside).
ńgwaka, person unfit for work.
ńgwalo, solicitation (of young girl).
ńgwě', mud seat.
ńgwẹl'anwu, iguana.

ṅgwẹle, mark round navel.

ñgwọ̀ (O), white spots of body.

ñ̈gwọ̀, *Raphia vinifera* (tree).

ñ̈gwọ̀, crab.

ṅgwụlọ, lame.

ṅgwụlọ̃ṅgwo, bad walker.

ñ̈kå', old.

ñ̈kå, carver (tool for ivory).

ñ̈kå, craftsman, clever.

ñ̈kåkǔ, shrew.

ṅkẹku, ṅkåkụ, foolish.

ṅkarume, "points" in game of akɓa.

ñ̈kạ̈tå (O), conversation.

ñ̈kǎtá, tree sp.

ñ̈kǎtá, fish sp.

ñ̈kạ̈tå, basket (round).

ṅkata ǎyiyọ, evil reports about some one.

(di) ṅkɓa, strong.

ṅkɓoloịča (O), bead (red and white).

ṅkɓonaka (O), ring.

ṅkɓonakoko, pleurisy, stitch.

ṅkɓoṅkɓọ̀zẹle (O), top (made of seed, no pin, no whip).

ṅkɓọnkpọ (A), stem left in ground.

ñ̈kɓụ, shaving head.

ṅkɓǔ, kokonut.

ṅkɓǔ, suffering loss (market closed).

ñ̈kɓú, anthill.

ṅkɓú, shouting.

ñ̈kɓú, woman's latrine.

ṅkɓuči, being silent.

ñ̈kɓudò (O), upside down.

ṅkɓulufie (A), bird species, all red (seen early morning).

ñ̈kɓuluko (A), seed of obwọgulu.

ṅkẹji, half broken.

ṅkẹlẹka, rag.

ṅkiko, fork for handing up building materials.

ṅkiliku, thicket.
íkǫ, sharp.
ñkǫ', wood.
íikǫ, sloping (straight) on side.
íkò, deep vessel.
íkò, forehead
ṅkò, dry—
 íkòkḃǫṅkò, dry wood.
ṅkolu, ready.
ṅkǫṅkǫ, whitlow (bad).
ṅkǫnǫ, larynx.
(di)íikṗǎ, narrow.
íikṗà, (A) need; careful [or ṅkpača]—
 ǫdim ṅkpa, I need it.
ṅkṗá (A), pincers, tongs (blacksmith).
íikṗá, scarce, dear.
íikṗá, bird sp.
ṅkṗa ǎkwukwǫ, (many) leaves.
íikṗá akwukwǫ, herb.
ṅkṗača (A), careful, cleaning roast yams.
(di)ṅkṗafolo, narrow.
ṅkṗakana, trap (rat); (from palm tree).
ṅkṗakanǫke, trap (rat).
ṅkṗali, insult.
ṅkpama (As.), matchet.
ṅkṗavo, armpit.
ṅkṗeča (O), scraping (yams).
ṅkpęle (Al.), rods of guitar.
ṅkṗese, "key" to open native door.
ṅkṗesi (A), root above ground, bit of bush stem.
ṅkṗęsiakoko (A), rib.
íikṗí, he goat.
ṅkṗįliaka (O), elbow.
ṅkṗiolo, small snail (A).
ṅkpilįte, pepper mortar.
ṅkpimwǫ, goat devoted to mwǫ; false step (O).
íikpǫ, peg.

ṅkpọ, small bottle.

ṅkpŏbe, embracing.

ṅkpọdimi, disease of nose.

ṅkpọdụ, basket (round) for keeping fish, etc.

ṅkpọfe, short road (A), (O).

ṅkpọfolo (A), fly or ant (2 species); (2) featherless (arrow), As.

ṅkpog' ilo (As.), grassy border of street.

ṅkpógọ, bent, serpentine (line).

ṅkpọgo, parapet, fence of sand (on road).

ṅkpọg' oke, boundary heap.

ṅkpogoṅkpo, heap.

ṅkpọkọ, beam of loom.

ṅkpọkọ (Ala), winding board.

ṅkpŏkpolo (Al.), ball.

ṅkpọ́kò, matches.

(onye) ṅkpokolo imi, one who talks through his nose.

ṅkpọlaka, man who has lost finger (nail); fowl.

ṅkpọ́li, (A) levelling with hoe.

ṅkpolo (atọ), strand of cotton.

ṅkpọ̀lọ́ (A), stocks (prisoner, madman), handcuffs, rod.

ṅkponirhu, cross lines on forehead (face marks).

ṅkponirhu, circlet (for head).

ṅkpọṅkpọ, short.

ṅkpọṅkpọ, ruined house.

onye ṅkpọnkpo imi, one who talks through his nose.

ṅkpọ́pu, foot disease.

ṅkpọpu, boring.

ṅkpọru, sloping.

ṅkposẹṅgo (O), rib.

ṅkpọ̀tá, coming out of ambush.

ṅkpọto, noise.

ṅkpu, shout.

ṅkpu, ant ḥeap.

ṅkpu, blunt.

ṅkpu, bundle.

ṅkpu (Ub.), stone—

 ṅkpu mẹji, the obi is dead (stone is broken).

ńkp̣ụ́kp̣ụ́, walking bent (as old man); hunch, hump (top of .back); rheumatism, chronic.

ńkp̣ụ́kp̣ụ́, man whose property is confiscated.

ńkp̣ụ́kp̣ụ́, beckoning.

ńkp̣ukp̣ùmẹ̀, red like venous blood.

ńkp̣ụlụ, piece, seed.

ńkp̣ụlogwugwu, root.

nkp̣ụrụ mili, drop (of water), hailstone.

ńkp̣ụlose, thick, strong hair, very curly.

ńkp̣ụlắmu (A), testicles.

(onyẹ) ńkp̣ụ lẹgo nal' ẹze, star that wanted to take king-ship (from the moon).

ńkp̣ụligwe, hail.

ńkp̣ụl' irhu (I.A), cross (mark) on face.

ńkp̣ụlive (A), bead.

ńkp̣ụlíyi (A), small stone (thief swallows one as ordeal).

ńkp̣ụlŏbì, heart—

ńkp̣ụlobi fẹpuli fẹpu, his heart fled away (i.e., his heart was in his mouth) (O).

ńkp̣ụlụbosi, day (counting one by one).

ńkp̣ụlụči, sticks representing či.

ńkp̣úlú, bed of yam (in field).

ńkp̣uluge (Al.), lobby of house.

ńkp̣umaka, white ants' nest.

ńkp̣úmè, stone.

ńkp̣uńkp̣u, shelter, shade.

ńkp̣ụ ńkp̣ụ̀, short.

ńkp̣ụ̀wa (A), fork, for handing up materials for house building.

ńkụ, oil palm (As.).

ǹkú, wing.

ńkufẹle, present (of wood).

ńkukọba, panting.

ńkúkù, fool, idiot, nonsense.

ńkùkù (A), corner (hollow) of box.

ńkulu, taking a child from another.

ńkwá, dislocation of shoulder.

ṅkwato ụ̣kwụ, hoof.

ṅkwẹbe, warp.

onye ṅkwẹnkwe, naive.

n̈kwọ̣ (O), saw.

n̈kwọ̣, fish ring (i.e., dried fish).

ṅkwolo (Og.), seducer of married woman.

ṅkwọmi (arụ), smooth skin.

ṅkwonye (Ub.), go between (suitor).

ṅkwụde, grater.

(iwu) ṅkwukwu, foolish.

ṇ̇kwụ, (As.) oil palm.

ṅo, (1) swallow ; (2) drink in big gulps.

ṅo n'ikili, swallow without biting (hard thing).

nṭọ́, ashes.

n̈tọ (A), ashes.

ṅtọ̣, breaking promise, failure to perform engagement.

ṅwa, try.

ṅwa ike, try hard.

ṅwa aǰadu, bastard.

ṅwa akṗata kṗata, bastard.

ṅwa dimwọ, changeling.

ṅwa di n'ọdọ, person with many relatives.

ṅwa imi ani (A. O), flat nose.

ṅwa kṗokili kṗokili, small child.

ṅwa ṁbia, (young) bushfowl (red legs).

ṅwa mili, urine.

ṅwa mwadụ, freeborn.

ṅwa ṅkpama ofu iru, child with only one freeborn parent
    (child of a matchet with one edge).

ṅwa nuku nuku, small child.

ṅwa ọiyi, bastard.

ṅwa uǰuǰu, bastard.

ṅwábiali, quiet.

ṅwabu, quiet.

n̈wåḃú, kill secretly.

ṅwačiẹfo ẹfo, (O), moth.

ṅwãda okḃulukui (I. A), oldest woman born in a quarter.

ṅwadibe, slave, servant.

ṅwakp̣a', fœtus.

onye ṅwamadi, man who marries rich woman.

ṅwambwǫko (Uk.), baby that does not cry.

ṅwandu̧, child (up to 5).

ṅwanikp̣a, name of dance (at Asaba).

ṅwata (pl. umwaka), child (up to 18).

ṅwata omajijiji, child that always shakes.

ṅwãza, sleeping-place outside *okule*.

ṅwę, burn (lamp).

ṅwę *li*, change.

(iru) ṅwelie, change colour.

ṅwe oṅwe, be free.

nwę́bu (nwa̧bu), quietly.

ṅwęfę, have over.

ṅwefi, calf.

ṅwetęte, small lizard (O).

ṅwo, change—

   ęṅwoęm, I change.

   ęṅwom, I changed.

ṅwo alisia, touch all over.

ṅwoli, resemble parent.

ṅwǫmi, lizard (striped).

ṅwomi, imitate.

ṅwŏmikalo, small striped lizard.

ṅworue, change—

   ęṅworum, I change.

   ęṅworuęm, I changed.

ṅwu̧, catch.

ṅwu̧, catch.

ṅwu̧, get share (land), chase (game), drink (palm wine), borrow.

ṅwu̧', die—

   áṅwu̧m, I die.

   áṅwŏám, I died.

   ǫṅwuru n'ototo, (child) died young.

       ,,    n'efifie, (man) died in early manhood.

ṅwụ aṅwụ, die.

ṅwụ iyi, borrow iyi, take oath.

ṅwụ ṅkpụlụ, remove nuts, remove grain of corn.

ṅwụ ikẹlẹgu, be surprised.

ṅwụ n'oinya, be caught in trap.

ṅwụ so ọṅwu, (child) play with adult.

ṅwụ̃' ụla, sleep from home.

ṅwụ̃ ụṅwụ', shine, be white.

ṅwube, shine in.

ṅwube ạinya, close eyes (disgust).

ṅwučapu, be quite clean.

ṅwuči, dazzle.

ṅwučita, dazzle.

ṅwụk' aṅwụkọ, thank (?).

ṅwúlạpu, open eyes.

ṅwụlụ, catch.

ṅwụlia, be glad.

ṅwunye - okṗoro, woman " married " by another woman.

ṅwụnye ọlụ, be half dead.

ṅwụpụ, take away.

ṅwụpụ aṅwụpụ, die.

ṅwụta ọ́sa (A), bring home wanderer.


o (Asaba) is often replaced by ọ (Oniča).

ồbã̈, good (also, he enters).

ồbã̈' (O), increase.

ö̃bá', menstruation.

ồbå, dancing for mwọ.

ọbabala, broad water.

ọbala, (1) bark of ọlọ ; (2) hard part of palm fibre.

ọ̃bålå, piece of palm branch.

ọbalobwi (Ub.), part of road trodden firm.

ọbe, rope ladder.

obe, cross.

ồbě, rafter (roof tree to wall).

ồbě, loom-post.

ȯbẹ́lé, bird species.

(di) ọbẹl' ọlụ, not difficult.

ȯbị (ẹ̀ji amaji), stick, long, for making a hole for yam stick.

ȯbị (A), heart, fathom.

ȯbị, living, dwelling.

ȯbị, king.

ọ̀biȧ, wax, etc., for rubbing ivory anklets ;
    wax, to stop leaky calabash (ọ̀biȧ, he comes).

obia, tree (big, used in building).

ȯbiȧ (A), stranger.

ọbĭáme, stranger.

ọbiȁǹgu, vulture.

obiaše (O. O), red yam.

ȯbịbị ȯwȧ, one who spoils the world, disturber of the peace.

ȯbịbị ȯwȧ, mole (on body), mark.

obi idẹgẹle (Ubuluku), pigeon.

ọ́bọ̣, sheath.

ọ́bọ̣, hole, palm of hand.

ọ̀bọ̈ mwọ̣, hole behind collar bone, [also ubwonu (of sick or thin person)].

ọ̀bọ̣, revenge.

ọ̀bọ̣, trench trap (O).

ọ̀bọ̣ (kpalonyedi), fish species.

ọ̀bọ̣, lazy, laziness.

ȯbọ̣', guitar.

ȯbȯ (O.), spear with lozenge-shaped head.

ȯbȯ (A) (false) accusation—
    ȯbȯlụ̀ m obȯ, he accuses me.

ȯbȯ, fish guts.

ȯbȯ, heap.

ȯbȯ ọko, furnace.

ọboba, worthy.

ọbobọ, pied (cloth), spotted.

ọ̀bóbȱ, worm.

ọ̀bȯ̆bo, drizzle.

obobwaṅkǫno, larynx.

ǫbǫdǫ, spear.

obóji, yam leaf.

ǫ̀bǫ̀kå, spotted.

ǫbǫka, open handed.

obokǫ, he goat that does not grow.

ǫbǫlagwa, spotted.

ŏbolo, deep water.

ǫbǫmpi, curious, inquisitive man.

obosi (a)na, 4.0—5.0 p.m.

obǒto ǫko, live coal.

obotǫko, embers.

ǫbu (su), offensive speech.

òbų̀, necklet.

òbù, deep (water).

òbù áјå, heap of mud.

obuba (O. O), cloth with two broad stripes.

ŏbůbwå, clay plate.

obŭle, torch.

obulu, open space (impluvium) in house.

obŭlu, brain.

obum, open stretch of sand, sandbank.

obute ǫka, a red yam.

obwa' (Ub.), old farm.

òbwá, sap of palm tree.

òbwå, (O), calabash.

ǫ́bwå (A), barrier, fence.

ǫ̀bwå, hole to plant yam.

ǫ̀bwå, palm flower.

ǫ̀bwå, stocks.

ǫbwa ageliga (A), kind of spear with oval head.

obwabwa, line, procession.

obwaga (I. A), yam species.

ǫbwakƀo, flesh.

obw' ák̇ú, palm nut before husking.

ǫbwánči, ceremonial staff.

ǫbwanike, cross stick to support calabash for palm wine.

ǫbwańkpi, stink ant.

ǫbwańkpi nna, ant.

obwanokoko, long pipe.

ǫbwapia, tall and thin.

ǫbwaru, down river, south.

òbwę̌', "garden egg."

òbwě', head of palm nuts, pine apple, etc.

òbwę̌ (A), quarter.

òbwě, cake, loaf of cassava.

òbwě akụ (O), bunch of palm nuts.

òbwě ńkpú, nut of koko palm (so too, sub-quarter).

òbwě odala, fruit (lime, mango, orange).

ǒbwě', bird sp.

ǒ̃bwě, market.

obwę litęle, diarrhœa.

obwębwę (O. O), snare.

(ndi) obwei (A), see Part III, p. 269, ndi ekwensu.

obwęle (Al., Id. U.), head of ịkpála.

obwęlęntili, prolapsed bowel.

obwi ǫnụ, silent; slow talker.

ǫ̇bwǫ́, company (As., Ala, Ib., Opp.).

ǫ̇bwǫ, circle (of dance).

ǫbwǫmwǫ, halo (sun or moon).

ǫbwǫ obodo, figures drawn on ground for Nkpetime.

obwǫ ozu, hole cut in tree for making palm wine.

òbwǒ, enough.

òbwǒ, winding board for thread, measure of cloth.

òbwǒ (A), situtunga (kind of antelope).

òbwǒ, woman's ring net.

ǫ̇bwǒ' (O), lufa (washing fibre).

obwodi, ignorant.

ǫbwǫdǫ (I.A., O. O), ceremonial spear.

ǫbwǫlǫ, calabash (O. O).

o bwǒlo, heifer.

ǒbwolo, crosspiece of ikum fence.

obwolońkita, knot, running knot to hold.

ǫbwǫńuke, ill luck.

ǫbwǫtu (O. O), lane cut for battue.

obwumbwada (H.), ? eagle.

ȯčĭ (? 4–1), bleeding calabash.

ȯčĭ, palm wine maker.

ǫčĭčĭ, darkness, dark—

 ǫčĭčĭ åbwȧ, darkness comes.

očo (I.A.), ill-luck (?), pollution (?).

očokǫlǫko, brand (fire).

očokolȯme, adult (25–30).

ǫda, mixture from *ube* for rubbing ivory anklets.

ǫdȧ, umbrella.

ǫdȧ, swirl, current.

ȯdȧ, bang, noise (of gun).

ȯda', " spice."

ǫdafi, rich man (As.); master, *i.e.*, husband (As.).

ȯdė, worthless.

odędẽle, loop of cotton (in spinning).

ȯdĭ, trench (for war, hunting).

odi, whole, unbroken.

odibwe (As.) [= ejĭje], bead (put in mouth of cze at burial).

odide mili, rumbling of rain.

odĭdi, big.

odido, spider.

odído, making peace.

ǫdĭkȧ, not—

 ǫdikȧbia, he has not come.

odinabǫ, midnight (O).

ǫdǫ, clump (of bananas), palm trees.

ǫdǫ, pool.

ǫdȯ, ivory.

ǫ̈dȯ, ivory, horn.

ǫdȯ, (O), tail.

ǫ̈dȯ, place in market.

ǫdȯ, warning, advising, threatening, quarrelling with.

ǫdo ębwe, incisors, middle, of upper jaw.

ȯdȯ, plant (= Bini afǫ).

ódò, peace.

ŏdò, (O), mortar.

ọ̃dódó, make weight.

ọ̃dódó, living tree or plant.

ọ̃dódò, pot of oil.

ŏdŏdò, mauve dye.

(ẹwu) odokŏdo, Hausa (goat); object from up river.

odozi, open place.

odudu, cold place (without fire)—

　dine n'odudu, sleep without fire.

ọdum (O), lion—

　ọdụm ẹdẹbu ụgụ anụ, lion never half kills animal.

odume,? leopard sp.

odumŏdu, soup, not boiled.

ódủṅwa, lost child.

ófå (Ogw. and H.), [= akete], tree, fibre used for cloth.

ófå, good luck.

ọ́fẹ̌, free gift.

òfẽ', gravy, soup.

ofẹfe, cloth.

(onye) ofẹke, one who does not understand subject, one who is not a doctor.

ofẹle, quick.

ofẹl' ọna, dangerous place (where there is a trap) (he passes, goes home).

òfï, seed used for food (H.).

ŏfi, yaws.

ofido, cross piece for spout for palm wine.

ofiẹge (On. ufiẹge), crossbeam.

ŏfiẹge, ridge-pole.

ọfịfi, whistle.

ofịli, ceiling (used for corn).

ofìọ, leg-hook (wrestling).

ọ́fọ́, doing something that shows love to parents.

ọfọ, stick for oath, etc.

ọ́fǒ, new.

ọ̀fọ̀, fish sp.

ọfọdo ṅwantikili, almost.

ọfofo, break of day.

ọ̀fọ̀fọ̀, foam.

ofokpọlọ, lungs.

ofọlo, vain, useless.

ọ̀fọlọ, canoe-pole (bamboo).

ofu, grievance.

ọ̀fụ̀, seer, prophet.

ọ̀fụfụ̀, disease like craw-craw.

ọga (ẹkw ọga), sewing—
    tu ọga, stitch 2 cloths with space between.

ọga, divider.

ọga, a girl's game.

ọ̀gá (As.), spear (barbed).

ọ̀gá (efi), track.

ọ̀gả', bush cane, creeper.

ọ̀gả', king's house, large obulu.

ọ̀gả' (ẹnu, ani), molar, corner of jaw.

ọ̀gả, inside of the house.

ogali (H.), knife.

ọ̀gả̀b́wa, jawbone.

ọ̀gả̀zụ̀, guinea fowl.

ọ̀gẹ̀, week ; time, more than 2 izu—
    eṅwẹlụm ọ̀gẹ̀, I have time.

ọgẹlẹga, rib.

ogẹli; ogali (H), knife.

ọgẹligazụ́ (A), spine.

ọgẹ́nàzụ́ (O), spine.

ogẹne, boundary heap (in farm), row.

ogẹn' ilo, edge of street.

ogịdịbwa, ladder.

ọgiga, passable.

ọgịgọ, denial.

ogịlịge, či (q.v. in Part IV).

ogịne (O. O), enemy.

ọ̀gịnị̀, rat, striped (*Arvicanthis striatus*).

Q̃gọ̀, relative-in-law.

ọ̃gọ̀', kindness, present.

Q̃gò, hoe—
　　fȧjì ọ́gò ọ̀gò wẻlȧnụ̀ ọ̀gò, they take twenty hoes for
　　war.

ọ̀gȫ' (O), twenty.

ọgo ili kwasi nnụ (I. A), six hundred.

ọgo ili, 200 cowries.

ọ̀gò' (A), fighting (between umunna, etc., no guns).

ọ̀gò, rat.

ògò, size.

ògò, rank (rich man).

ògȫ, buyer.

ògò, farm.

Q̃gọ̀dọ̀, mud hole.

Q̃gòdò, pool.

Q̃gògò', hoarse.

ogoli, married woman; a woman who quarrels with her
　　husband calls him di ogoli; the man calls her di
　　ogoli ṅwainye.

ọgọ̃nọ', sword, bent.

ogọṅgoleta (O), wife's sister's husband.

ogonzu (Ob.), lump of chalk.

ọ̃gụ̀, (it is) finished.

ọ̀gụ̀, medicine.

ògụ̀, splinter, thorn, fish spine.

ògụ̀, crowd.

ògụ̀, tally (of things sent to father-in-law).

ògụ̀dụ̀, deep water.

ogudu (ọifia), depths (of the bush).

ọ̃gụ̀dụ̀, since.

ogùgù, pit, hole (O, A), well of water.

ogugu, numerable, to be counted—
　　fa dirọ Q̃gùgù, they are innumerable.

ògùgù, Ogugu alose.

ogugu ani, people sent to aj̈oifia (? Okp.).

ògulugu, trunk, body.

ogumagana, chameleon.

ǫgwǎ, fish sp.

ǫgwǎ, tree sp.

ǫgwǎ (? 4–1), front house.

ǒgwę̌', trunk of tree (big); tree, fallen.

ǒgwę̌, "royalty" on catch of fish in other man's water.

ǫyǫm, accidental homicide.

ǫhǫliobo (A), bamboo.

ǫičaba, half ripe.

ǫi čanoji, black and white.

oifia ǫkb̌o (O. A), uncut bush.

ǫififi' aǰa (A), last section on top of wall.

ǫinyǎ, injury, sore.

ǫinyǎ, trap, web (spider's).

ǫinyǎ, friend.

oinyâzu, sore (back).

oinyịlum (O), enemy.

ǫiya olo (On.), liar.

ǒiyịlia, part of head of palm nuts.

ǫǰa, people.

ǫǰǎ, flute.

oǰa, great, much.

oǰala, noise.

oǰęle, tall (palm tree).

ǫǰǐ, kola, part of bride price.

ǫǰi alia, white kola.

ǫǰi aṅwe, "elastic" kola.

ǫǰi odi, kola that cannot be broken.

ǫǰǐ, iroko.

ǒǰǐ, doctor's staff.

ǒǰǐ, black.

oǰi odafe ukwe, yam species.

ǒǰǐ oko, plantain.

oǰigǐpu, palm nuts, soft (hardly any kernel).

oǰiji, mutual "cutting," quarrel.

ǒǰǒ,' pawpaw (*Papaiya*).

ǒǰǒ,' canoe wood.

onye ọǰugalo, slow goer.
oǰụ̈ǰu, full.
oǰuǰu olulu, bundle of cotton.
(onye) ọǰu mọli, slow goer.
oǰune, enemy.
ọ̊kå (A), Awka (town).
ọ̊kå (A), corn, maize—
faǰi ọka lat' ọkoko, they take corn to catch a fowl.
ọ̊kå, ant (? white).
ọ̊kå, wise man, clever man—
ǒnyě ọ̊kå mwåde nåtå ọ̊kå n'ọ̊kå', a wise man eats corn at Awka.
ọ̊kå, old.
ọka agwẹgwe, flour.
ǒkå, liar—
ǒkå m̀wådǒ nåtå ọ́kå n'ọ̊kå', a liar is eating corn at Oka.
ǒkå, bad (taste).
ǒkå, rest day.
ǒkå, backbiting.
ọkači, poison (for arrow or bullet); viper's head and tail, abwẹsi, and ground nut.
okakb̄a, long broom.
ọkala, quarter of a bushel.
ǒkålå, side of farm.
ọkam, force—
n'ọkam by force (kwa ife).
ọkånde, delicate, always sick.
okåwu, fish sp.
ọ́kb̄a, fence between ikum net and tower.
ọ́kb̄å, shuttle.
ọ̊kb̄à (A), foot, leg.
ǒkb̄å, seed used as kola—
onye t' okb̄a la mili omwalu k'enu di, a man eats okb̄a, and drinks water; he knows how the world is.
ǒkb̄å, perseverance.

ȯkƀå, red mud.

ȯkƀå, basket (long).

ȯkƀå', climbing rope (made of ạbo, bush rope).

okƀa ikum, loop for standing on in working ikum.

okƀaka, shoulder.

ȯkƀ̈ålå, splash.

okƀala okukwe, rod used in the loom.

ȯkƀ̈ånå, butterfly.

ǫkƀandide (Al.), swift (bird), n.

ǫkƀánka, next (worker).

ǫkƀatu (Ub.), snail species.

okƀe, monkey species; white under eye.

ókƀìlì, "horn"; calabash.

ǫ̇kƀǫ̇, fish sp., (ǫ́kƀǫ̇, he calls).

ǫ̇kƀǫ̇, fist.

ȯkƀǫ̇, for ever.

ǫ̇kƀǒ', fish sp.

ǫ̇kƀǒ, target.

ókƀǫ, (? red) yam wrapped in leaf, grated and beaten (O. O).

ókƀǫ̇, corn, etc., balls.

ȯkƀǫ̇, fufu.

ȯkƀǫ̇, dwarf.

ókƀǒ, long time.

ȯkƀǒ, slip (of foot).

ȯkƀǒ, burning.

ȯkƀǒ, worm (intestinal).

okƀǫfufu, sweat.

nko ȯkƀǒkƀå, log.

okƀokǒlo, a white yam.

okƀolo, single (thing).

ǫkƀolokƀo, meat without bone.

ǫkƀolǫkƀo akƀo, lump, tumour.

ókƀolukƀu, bottom (wood) of basket.

okƀonjęle, careless.

okƀǒnto, grey.

okƀonu, bachelor.

okɓosilo, image like ikeṅga.

okɓǫtǫ, 3 line pattern with thick thread.

ǫkɓụtǫlǫkɓu, everlasting.

okɓu, grasshopper.

okɓú, hat.

ókɓú, bush cat.

ókɓǔ, cover.

okɓu ani, water that runs underground.

okɓu ani (A), uncultivated edge of farm ; in second year
  planted with corn.

okɓukɓontǫ, green.

òkɓúkɓu, upside down.

okɓulu, sitting on eggs.

ǫkɓunẹkwe, back of neck.

okɓwǫsi, staff for sick person.

(di) oke, adversary, adulterer.

ǒkẹ́, boundary, peg.

òkě, male, big—
  íkè gu oke efi, ogǫrǫ mpu ye ainya, if an old bullock
  is tired, he bends his horn to close his eyes.

oke ẹbo, oldest man in ẹbo.

oke efifie nabǫ, midday.

oke olili, glutton.

òkě, share.
  oke olurǫ (m), I got no share.

òkě, rat—
  òkě ïwókě tiṅyěl òkě nòkòkě, male rat put peg to
  mark share.

ókefi, bull.

okei, adult (30–40).

okei ani, adult (40 upwards).

okei ẹbo, elder.

okëke, interfering person.

ǫkẹlẹkẹtǫ, edge of branch (palm).

ǫkẹlẹkp̀a, black teeth.

(di) okẹmina, deep, profound.

ǫkẹni (Al.), "friend."

òkĕso (O), boil.

okẹte (Al.), palm tree.

onye ọkikă abwa, other party to an agreement.

ọkikabwa, one who makes an appointment (to meet).

ọkikọ, drying.

okiko, sewing breadths of cotton together.

okiko, (Ib.) beam, used for storing corn.

ŏkĭlĭ (O), guinea corn.

òkĭlĭ, iron armlet.

ŏkiliko, net ring.

òkiliko, snare.

ony' ọkọ, go-between (suitor's).

ọ́kŏ, fishing.

ŏ̃kŏ, riches.

ọ̀kŏ, pipe.

ókọ̀, message.

òkọ̀, creeper sp.

òkọ̀, dear.

òkọ̀, cloth (from bamboo).

ókŏ, hole in bank of river.

ókŏ, head of corn, husk of kola.

ókŏ, (Al.) parrot.

òkŏ, male—

    akƀo ƀiyi, óji bul' ŏko, cotton tree is oath alose, ir oko
      is male, i.e., greater.

ókò, a white yam.

òkŏ', full power.

òkŏ, sticks for hanging net to dry.

òkŏ (I.A.) boy.

ọ̀kụ̆, fire.

okọ̀iyẹlia, sub-head of nuts.

ọ̀kọ̀ji, irritation caused by yam juice.

ọkokabwa, (O) person whom one has arranged to call by
    another name.

okokƀolomwọ, old bachelor.

ọkọkọ (O. O), unripe palm nuts.

ọ̀kŏkŏ, planting.

ǫkoko nanąba (ala), evening meal.

okokume, lung.

okokwe, a white yam.

ǫ̈kǫli útulú, necrosis of septum of nose or nose bones.

ǫkolo, okro.

ŏkŏlŏ, gun shield (of skin).

òkŏ́lŏ́, boy.

ŏkǫ̀m, yam sp.

okoṅgu, ǫkǫṅgu, bent (wood, iron).

okoti ǫnụ, mark at corner of mouth.

ǫkǫtǫ, creeper sp.

ǫ̇kṗǎ, quarter staff.

ǫ̇kṗa odi, cock that has not crowed.

ǫkṗ akęlęka, half grown oil palm with leaves (the same size as akiti).

(ani) okṗa, red sand.

ǫkṗalumunna, elder, head of umunna.

ǫkṗalidumu, elder, head of idumu.

ǫkṗalębo, elder, head of ebo.

(di) ǫkṗi, niggardly.

ǫ̇kṗǫ̀, name sake.

ǫ̇kṗǫ̀, fish sp.

okpŏ̌ fulu, yam sp.

okṗŏfulu, careless.

ǫkṗokṗǫ azu, spine.

ǫkṗǫl' irhu (Ala), forehead marks.

okṗolo, clay.

ŏkṗolo osisi, trunk.

okṗom ǫkụ, warm.

okṗonu, orphan without brother or sister.

okṗoro ani, (I.A.) head woman of idumu.

diokṗoro, woman who " marries " another woman.

ǫkṗò uzǫ, centre of road.

ǫkṗukṗa, (1) plot (in farm); (2) line dividing plots.

ǫkṗukṗǫ abwaka, humerus.

ǫkṗukṗǫ ęgǫlǫ, tibia.

ǫkṗukṗǫ obi, breast bone.

ọkp̣ukpọ ọbwọdọbwọ, femur.

ọkp̣ukp̣o uḳwu, pelvis.

okp̣ulu (Og.), small basket.

n'okp̣ulu, under.

okp̣unẹkwe, back of head.

okp̣wili mili, situtunga horn.

ọ̀kụ̀ (Al.), call, word.

ọ̀kụ̀, a red yam.

oku ji oiča, a red yam.

okuikui (Al.), owl.

ọ̀kụ̀jì, high Niger.

ọ̀kụ̀jì, bird species (sings in early morning).

okukŏlo, unripe nuts.

okukume, ? diaphragm, inhaling.

okule, store room.

okulutu, fish species.

ọ̃kụ̀mụ́, lame.

ọ̀kụ̀mwọ̣, place of alose(?) in farm.

okuzu, wild sheep (?), goat (?).

ọ̣kwá', plate (wood), vessel.

ọkwači, dish on which či is kept.

ọkwaṅkpẹle ụ ḳwụ, patella.

ịkwà̃, pan (for priming).

ọ̣kwà̃', francolin, bush fowl.

ọ̣kwà̃, widow.

ókwà̃, tree, *Treculia sp.*, bread fruit.

ọ̀kwá, condition.

ókwẹ̀, throwing of balls, knucklebones.

ọ̀kwè̀, leaf.

ọ̀kwề, bean (black).

okwịbo (Okp.), bush fowl.

ọkwọ, fist.

ókwò̀, yam leaf blown off by wind.

okwode, path (in farm).

okwọtọ (O. O), cloth with double warp.

ọkwŭkwọ, baling.

okwukwu, (Al.) owl.

ǫkwulo, okro.

òkwûlû, stomach.

ólå, state.

ólá, slap.

ólá, sleep, sleeping.

ólå (O), ruse.

ólå, tree species, *Bridelia ferruginea.*

ǫle', a white yam.

olẹ̀ge, beam, ridge pole (?).

olẹlimwǫ (Ib.), unburied corpse.

ólî, corn paste; corn boiled in oma leaf.

ólî (H), ointment (nut oil and koko leaf).

ólî, yam sp.

ǫlie (mwadu), sickly.

olifala fala, disease (causes sores).

olie (O. O.), human figure drawn in chalk on the road for magic.

olifie, (O) bird sp., red.

olila, green snake.

olilinwa, false pregnancy (or miscarriage *ca.* five months).

ǫlilǫ, snake sp. (slender, green).

olîló, pain.

oliǫma, day for worship of mother (day after Iwaji).

oliǫ ǫtitǫ, spot (on cloth).

oliufie, bird sp., sings, red breast.

ólǫ́, cheap.

ólǫ, clay.

ǫ̀lǫ̀, withered hand, disease that causes leg to wither.

ǫ̀lô anu, hind quarter (animal).

Olǫ, feast; throw firewood on water in July; in Asaba every two years; to drive sickness; can't take water from river that day.

   in Ibuzǫ; throw in ajoifia.

ólô, cunning.

óló' (=alo), abominable, forbidden.

ólô, shot gun.

ólô, bad action.

òlǒ, long pipe.

olo, acquittal—

   orainyeli olo, he is not guilty.

ọlọbwa, knock kneed, crooked, walker, feet.

ọlọ̆ji, jealous of—

   ọ́lọ́jǐ nåkwẹ,

ọlọko, comet.

ololi (Al.), lucky.

ọlọlo, lucky.

olǒlo, quick.

ololo akᵬo, tumour, hard.

ọ̀lọlọbwọ, python ; fabulous animal.

ologoze (Ub.) yam species.

ọlọlumwọ (As.), ukbo for či.

ọ̆lóse, bird sp.

ọ̆lụ̆, work.

(di) ọlụ, difficult.

òlú, Olu (ólů̀=he reaches).

òlů, a white yam.

òlǔ, riverside (people).

òlú, turn (to do).

olu nibwo, "opposite sides " in game of akᵬa.

olǔči, helpless.

olukṗulu, blindfold.

olukṗǔlu, very small (child).

olulu, rotten (wood).

olulu ifulifu, strand of cotton.

olulu ofolo, sewing cotton.

oluru ofe, bad soup.

ọma, lock (of hair).

ọma ikᵬọ, yam species.

òmå ǰi, yam just growing from seed.

òmá, leaf for thatch.

omafu, yam species.

ọmago (A), farm, farm land.

(ṅwata) omaǰijiǰi, cheeky boy.

ọmaṅgǎna, one who sits in one place.

ọmé (O. O), well.

ome ko ẹme, one who causes confusion.

ọmẹlẹmi, long (road).

ọmẹzi, if not (it does not).

ɔmị, yam sp.

ɓmị' (osisi), marrow, middle of bone, tree pith.

ọmikọ (nwọmi), lizard sp.

omilọ ( = ṅwọmi), lizard sp.

omɔfu, way of doing things.

ọmǔ, market queen.

ọmǔ ani, bottom, marsh.

ọmǔ, current.

ọmùmwǎ, whetstone.

omumatu, example.

ọmụmụ̌, fruitful woman.

ọm ụmụ̣, learning.

ọmùmù, current.

ọmǔmǔ, sharpening.

omwapalipali, greedy.

omwata, well behaved.

òmwǎ (nya, eči), at the same time.

ọnabwa (Al.), small house.

(di) onazayụ, noisy, troublesome.

onani (O. Oz.), granary.

onenone, few.

ọnina, snatching.

onine, plank over door.

onini, oath place.

ọninọ, elastic.

ọnọ', rat (brown).

ọnọdò, seat.

onogo, corn store (As.).

onoko, water yam sp.

ọnọkọ, cloth.

ọnọ̈kọ, matchet.

ɔnoku, a yam species.

onɔli, man who offends obi (Id. U).

onoli, patch (1) left uncleared; (2) planted with corn only.

ọnono, long calabash.

ọ̀nʼọ́nọ̀, fidgetty man.

ọnono nwẹzọ̌bolo, lozenge marks on forehead.ʼ

onono, straight road.

onozi, (1) person without genitals, either male or female; (2) man with testicles removed [in Hinterland, to make slave grow].

Onozi, priest in Asaba.

ọ̀nụ̣, mouth, price, cave.

ọ̀nụ̣ afia, price.

ọ̀nụ̣ ani, cheapness.

ọnụ̣ ụbwọ, bow of canoe.

ònụ̣, pit.

ònụ̣, neck.

onu ani, isthmus.

onu nta, high note.

onu uku, low note.

onududu, goitre (neck).

ọ̃nọ́mà (O), angry, wrathful.

(onye) onunu n̄jo, bitter person, bad person.

onyẹnye, female (quadruped).

ọ̀ṅwǎ, fish species.

ọ̃̀ṅwǎ, moon.

ọ̀ṅwotiti, moonlight (A. O).

òǹwệ, self.

oṅwẹ limba, girls' game.

ọ̀ṅwụ̣, death.

ọ̀ṅwụ̣, child that runs crying to mother.

oṅwu, famine.

(aj̈ʼ) opa, red sand, red mud.

opi, long calabash, flute.

òpiʼ̌lò, basket fish trap.

ọ̀pọ̣, taking thing from brother (i.e., not stealing

ọ̃popo (O), new moon.

opunisi, crown of head.

ọ̀rå, all, people.

ọ̀rà, tree sp.

(onye) orepió, slow goer.

orẹwệ, slow goer.

orhẹṅwa, child (of first marriage or illegitimate) born in other ẹbo.

orhi, fungus, used in magic against theft.

ọ̀rhî, thief.

ọrira, fruiting.

ọ́rọ̀, vulva.

ọ̀rọ̀ (A), dregs.

ọ̀rọ̀ mîa (A), dregs of palm wine.

ọro ite, bottom of pot.

ọrụnọ (Obo.), latrine.

ọ̀rů, twenty.

ọ̀rú, slave.

ọ̀rů ọ̀rů ọ̀sọ̀, 20 runaway slaves.

ọ̀så, wide.

ọ̀så, snail.

ọ̀så, squirrel (small striped), *Funisciurus leucostigma talboti.*

osåka, vagabond, idler.

ósẹ̀ (A), pepper—
  onye avale ọgalainya, otag' ose, ota ọ̌ji, who is near rich man, if he does not eat pepper, eats kola.

ọ̀sẹ̀, friend.

ọ̀sẹ̀', rib.

ọ̀sẹ̀ (Abo.), water side.

ọ̀sẹ̀ (A), convulsions.

ọ̀sẹ̀, či (*q.v.*).

ọ̀siå, excuse.

ọ̀siå, greediness.

osiali (si), witness.

oside ọka, ropes for hanging corn (Obọmpa).

osiẹli, witness.

ọsiọsiọ, seed used by widow and doctor.

ọšiọwo, fish sp.

osîse, smoke.

osịse, drawing (up).
ọsisi, staff for worship of ancestor.
ŏsìsĭ, cooking.
ŏsîsĭ, tree.
ŏ̃sĩsĭ, measure.
osịte, tripod.
ọ̀sọ̀, running.
ọ̀sọ̀ (O), wanderer, lost child, foundling.
ŏsọ̀, sweetness.
ósŏ, ovary (fowl).
ŏ̃sŏ', bat (big), *Eidolon helvum*.
ŏsŏ̃', edge of bush, bottom of wall, tree.
oso ani, spit of sand, land.
ŏsŏ obwabwa, very long.
óso osŏ, second child.
ósŏ̃sŏ, next.
osodi ọka (Idum.), corn rope.
osogoli (Obo.), idler.
osŏkoto, youth (18 to 25).
ŏsŏkŭ, peg.
osolo, incisors of lower jaw ; outer ditto of upper jaw.
ŏ̃somà, loss (O).
ŏ̃sŏmė, disturbance.
ọsọso (=awẹli) (Ubul.), creeper used for making ṅgo.
ŏsŭ, sacred slave.
osukŭlu, young animal or person (up to 10).
ọ̃sŭsŭ isi, head dressed with hair high after taking title.
ọ̀šŏ (As.), vulva.
ọta, wish (Al.).
ọta, marching at burial or feast.
ọtã̃, favourite wife.
ŏt̞ặ (i̞t̞a), blame.
ŏt̞ặ, bow.
ota olulu, cotton bow.
ŏtå, company (work).
ọtakwu, widow's house.
otala (Abọ), food, fufu.

ọ̀tanjẹle, antimony.
ồt̟é, path.
ồté, payment.
otele, level.
ọtẹte, atẹte, basket tray.
ồtí', sickness.
ọtibwumbwada, obwumbwada (H), ? eagle
otirhi, fish fence.
ọ̀tìt̟è, distance.
ọ́tọ̀, long lived.
ọ́tọ̀, muddy.
ọ̀tọ̀' upright.
ọ̀tọ̀', naked.
ọ́tò (A), vulva.
ótồ, root of big tree (buttress used for door).
ồtồ, tendo Achillis.
ồtồ, praise.
ồtó, worm that eats fruit.
ồtŏbwồ, gown.
ọtolaka, horn, ivory.
ọtŏlo (O), tree sp.
ọ́tolo àgwà (A), spotted.
ồtŏlồ, fat.
ọtolu ọrhọlu, small boil that becomes big sore.
ọ̀toto (O), new moon.
ồtọ̀tŏ', flower.
ồt̟ŏt̟ồ, morning.
otu ịza, market place (months).
ótů (O), side of river, stream.
ồtú (O), society, company.
otu rhaza, see Part IV, p. 47.
ồtúm, canoe-pole.
ồt̟ǚt̟ồ (A), growing.
ŏtůtů, hammer, creeper sp.
ŏtůtů, blister.
ồtůtú (Isele), terrifying object.
ŏtůtů, fish-trap (drop), net.

otutu afa, dance name.

ồtútú or hi, tracking thief.

otụtụ (akpọba), hiccough.

ỗyửyử (O), loss.

ồwẵ, world.

ồwẳ, torch (fibre).

ọwẳlẳ, torch.

ówai (Al.) [= akƀoluku], leaders of workers.

owambo, the uruči of a man's či (q.v.).

owant'(a) ẹfifie, 11.0 a.m.

owe, quiet.

owo (Ani ọfo), (?) smell etc. of dead body.

ọwọli, creek.

ówử, touch wood (for soup).

ówử, fame, rumour.

ówử (O), cobra, spitting (naga).

ồwử, incised wound.

óyẳ', horse tail ; fly whisk (long).

óyẳ, cry.

ồyẳ, disappointment.

ồyẳ, unbearable ; insult.

oyada, ungrateful.

ồyẹlẻ, small hole.

ồyẹlẻ, hair in tufts.

óyỉ, resemblance.

ồyỉ, cold (noun).

óyỉyỉ, raw.

óyỉyỉ, good for nothing ; all dying, lost.

ọyọ, seed of odala (kernel); for dance anklets.

óyọ, easy.

ọzẳ, hair on animal's neck.

ọzạṅwu (A), sunshine (hot sun).

ozẹle, seed for spindle.

ozẹle olulu, spindle.

ọzỉ', tree sp.

ózỉ (A), message, house work.

ồzỉ, drum (big burial, cow skin, one end only).

ȯzi̥, straight.

ozi̥ge (ǫna), green pigeon.

ozinye (H), gum (from tree).

ǫziza (Okp.), bride price.

ọ̀zìza (O) or ọ̇zízȧ, lamentation.

ǫ̃zizȧ or ȯzîzȧ, sweeping.

ǫzɪ̃za, swelling, on foot or hand, bruise.

ǫzɪ̃za, answering.

ǫ́zǫ̇, chimpanzee (?).

ọ̇zǫ̇, another.

ȯzȯ, rain.

ȍzó, blacksmith.

ọ̇zȯa, foolish.

ǫzǫgɪ̃de, lease (?) rods (loom).

ȯzu̥, palm wine from felled tree.

ȯzu̇', corpse.

ozu' onini (Al.), unburied person.

ozubu ę̇wu, long haired goat.

ozugu nzugu, owl.

ȍzugwe, snake sp.: is ę̇zǫ̃gwǫ, king of snakes: red, black lines.

ozuzu, plot, esp. area cleared for farm and subdivided later.

ȯzu̥zũ, terrifying object.


pá, carry.

pado, lay down.

pago, carry to.

på̇i, interjection; disgust at bad luck.

pako ṅpako, be haughty.

pana, take some.

papu̥ta, carry out (living being)

pasę̇be ǫku̥, light fire.

pata, bring.

pé, be small.

pę̃, give.

pę̇lepę̇lę̇nti, lobe of ear.

pǫpe, take good care of.

pẹta, cut small piece.

pẹta, bear one or two children.

pị, peel—

    åpìm, peel.

    åpìä̈m, peeled.

    [I flog, ä̈pìåm].

pị ato, clean chewing stick; make payment to mother* of idẹbwe.

pị̈ (?), squeeze.

pí⁻, carve—

    p. åpìm; a. apiam.

pị̈, squeeze.

pị osisi, make of wood.

pị̈a apia, rot (beans, corn).

pìåm, not at all—

    (pìåm, whip me).

pị̀čá, shape.

pị̀čá', squeeze out.

pịde apide, make smooth.

pịẹtue, bring down by throwing at it.

pịlia apìlia, make smooth.

pilikitim, not at all.

pìǒ, (a. ẹpioẹm), force way through.

pǫ ǫpǫ, make oneself at home, take thing without telling owner.

pǫba, expose yams for sale.

pǫči pǫči afifia, low grass.

pǫdo, expose yams for sale.

pokǫ, visit.

pụ ala, be mad.

pụ ẹlo, (1) "live for ever," (2) grow fungus.—

    idu uče iga pu ẹlo, if you have sense, you live long.

    òpù ẹ̀lǒ: present.  òpùė ẹ̀lǒ: past.

pụ obi, emigrate.

pụ òkò, be able.

pụ ilẹ, spoil, lose strength.

pu n'ilo, pu n'ẹzi, go outside.
pu(gọ) n'ọlu, be free of work.
pu n'ụnọṅwa, cease mourning.
puča, clear from.
pugo (na), be unnatural; be out of health; finish being.
   ọpugọ na mwadu; he is out of health.
   —    — nne,      she is an unnatural mother.
puku, visit.
puku ọlili, visit.
pukute, visit.
pulu, snatch.
ifolo (a) puta, be light.
puta na, lead to (road).
pu, very bad (small).
pu ẹpu, leak, spring up.
pu n'ani (a), be native, spring up.
puči, replace, come up in place of.
puru, be half broken.


rå, bore hole.
rá, take with hand.
rá aṅwu, take honey.
rá ifulu, blossom.
ra iǰe, go a journey.
rá otaṅke, send spy.
rá ụkọ, send messenger.
rá ụkwụ, walk—
   ra si ụkwụ ike, walk fast.
ra ịgwa, walk "proudly," put on side.
rá, choose, be equal, march, comb, sound.
rå, pay fine.
rå, prevent, be weaned.
rå, release, leave (alone).
rå nrạinya, be equal.
ra amu, crack.
ra enye, settle matter.

rabã, develop seeds, fruit.

raɓu, neglect.

rạče, take before—

    ṅwá ạ́rạ̌čẹ̀ nṅả, son does not take before father.

    ṅwá ảrạ̌čẹ̀ nṅả, son takes . . .

rainye, pour into.

rậịnya, be equal.

råinyé alo, advise.

råinyé iịe, go slowly.

rainye ụ̣kwụ̣, walk slowly.

raịnyẹlu, put blame (on another).

rainyesili, leave altogether.

raka, act.

rålú, leave.

rálu, prefer, chose.

rálu alo, confer.

råsịlị, leave altogether.

ráta, choose one's fate.

rátinye, pour into.

rẹ̃, take.

reɣali, creep about.

renye ụ̣kwụ̣, walk slowly.

rẹpu (ụ̣nọ̣), take off (roof).

rha ikum, let down net.

rha ịi akwu, remove yams from the old farm.

rha ono, perform ceremony against ill-luck.

rhainye mwadụ̣, assign " friend."

rhainye okụ n'oifia (Og.), "take palaver to the bush"
    (kill adulterous wife of obi).

rị́, pull hard.

rị̣ (or ši) ama, mark.

rị̣ rinye (or ši šinye), stick fast.

rị̣ (or ši) ṅkp̀ụ̣, cry out.

rị̣, swell.

ri, be—

    ṅwa ẹrigunne, the child is big.

ri (a. ẹriẹm), leak.

rhi (Ala), (1) clean, (2) remove.

ri ṅwa (Ib.), wash new-born child.

ričapu, cleanse.

rįči, swell and fill, heal.

rįli, swell, heal.

rįnye, (p. & a. same), refuse to move.

rinye, hand over.

rįrapu, shine bright (sun).

riruka, move aside.

rọ́, arrange, lift.

ró, pull.

rọ́ (rụ́), roast.

rọ̆, shake, blow bellows, price.

rŏ̈, regret.

rọ̈ ụma, charge too much.

rọ̈ arụ, shiver.

rọ̈ ẹko, work bellows.

rọ̈ nni, fear.

rọ̈ ọnu, chatter (cold).

rọ̈ ọnụ, price.

rŏ̈, hang.

rŏ̈ iro, tell story in song (On.); regret, feel sad, think other-
    wise.

rŏ̈ mili, urinate.

robwu, hang person.

rọgo erọgolo, ascend.

roya eroya, transplant.

rokwo, picking unripe fruit.

rụča aji (ẹwu), singe off hair.

ru ani, sacrifice.

rú, pour, run.

rú (ṅwa) mili, urinate.

rú, bend.

rú, mourn.

rú uru, mourn.

rú adaru, flow down (hill).

rŭbe, (1) flow, (2) walk slowly.

rubęke, bend.
rubu, mix (liquid).
rudę, drift.
rudo, persuade.
ruę ęruę, pull out.
(iru) ruęli, (face) change.
ruęli ęruęli, turn over and over.
rúfu, pour away.
rugǫli, be proud.
rugo nrugo, be proud.
rugwa, mix (liquid).
rukp̃udo, turn upside down.
rukp̃udo, cover.
rukwasi, pour upon.
rulu ani, stoop.
runata ani, stoop.
runye, pour in.
ruyali, turn over.


sa, crawl.
sá, open eyes.
sá, spread open.
så, wash, answer.
sá afia, separate sheds with the loom sword.
sa iru, flat (country), (stone).
saba, unfold, open out.
sakb̃o, cover, (as hen her chicks).
sali, pick up.
sali ainya, open eyes.
sapo bwodo, flat (table).
sata (eǰune), collect (snails).
sé, stir; take photo; consult.
se, take away.
sé ęsẽ', draw, pull, photograph.
sé ę̇sė, make palaver.
sé, float.

sé afia, give money to buy goods.
se ámụmả, lighten; amuma sè, it lightens.
sé ẹsẹ̀, float.
sé ikum, pull up net.
sẹ ṁpala, walk with long steps.
sé use aši, put aside part of day's food.
sé utili, stretch self.
sebwa, form train, go on.
sečiya, draw back.
sẹka, pull asunder.
sẹkpu ụbwọ, overturn canoe.
sẹkpulu ani, kneel down.
sẹkpuni, lift up.
sẹkpunita, draw up.
sẹkpụnye, drag into.
sẹkpupu, drag away.
sẹnita, lift by force.
sẹputa, take out.
sẹpute, take out.
sẹsa, scatter.
sẹtẹ, bring.
sẹti, draw out.
sẹti arụ, stretch oneself.
sẹtipu, stretch.
sẹtipu ije, go quickly.
sẹtu, pull load from head, drag down.
sẹwa, tear.
sị, say—
    isi, you say (or you cook).
sị ifi, name corespondent.
sị oku, answer.
sị ȯsiả, be greedy.
šiči azu, go back.
šičiẹte, go back.
šido, (yam) choke.
sí, cover (bird, insect, snake, tortoise, lizard).
sí, pass.

si, get thick; ọlọ sia, the soup has got thick.

si, smell.

ṣi iṣi, smell.

si isi, smell—
    isi isi, you smell.

sí, pass—
    isigà, you pass.

si aiyadi—
    esim aiyadi, how am I ?

sí ike, be strong, do strongly.

sí ite, cook.

sí oke, be underdone (hard).

si ọbọ, be lazy, get lazy.

sí oinya, set a trap.

si šite, choose one's fate.

si', measure.

si ụnọ, trace out house.

siainye, teach medicine.

sibe ọgu, make medicine.

sibe ite, put pot on fire.

sibue, dye.

šịa ụšịa, shine.

sifẹ, pass.

sifie, take wrong road.

sika ike, be stronger.

sikƀo, uncock (gun).

sikƀu ụzọ, miss road.

sịkwu asi, calumniate.

sịli ṅkọ, crooked, sideways.

sine, compare.

siṅwu, scorch, wither.

siṅwuba iru, look disgusted.

sipụta, come out from.

siresi, be still uncooked.

sisa, put ground corn in water for bad to float.

sisọ, only.

sis' orhai (I.A), take out orhai (in burial).

site, through, since.

siwa, pain much ; break pot in cooking.

sọ́, please.

sọ, push, carry something on head against person, butt.

sọ mpi, butt.

sọ ṅgọṅgọ (ada), stumble.

ọsisọ sọ (H), sweat (verb).

sọ ṅsọ́, forbid.

sọ (osọ), please.

sọ́ ụsọ, be sweet.

sọ ainya, forgive.

sọ amụ, amuse.

sọ ìsì, walk as blind man.

sọ ọkụ, wave torch at person.

sọ' ume, consult.

só, grow—

   ǰim nẹso nenyem, I grow yams.

só arụ, be fat.

só, stitch.

só, bend fish on stick.

so mmwa, sharpen knife.

so ṅkp̣o, cut without leaving mark.

só n' ofu, be of same age.

só uso, (1) be long, be delayed, (2) grow long.

sŏ̃, follow.

so mbwambwa, very long.

sobata, (I.A) remove outlawry.

sobu nsobu, cause trouble.

s' ofu, only.

s' ofu nǰe, once for all.

solu, precede.

sonita, grow up.

sọpọ̀, faint.

sopo, excommunicate, send to Coventry.

sọpụlụ, honour.

sọrụ, faint; be nearly dead.

sọ́si, follow out.

sǫsǫ, only.

sote ǫmali, grow up and know (sign).

sotu, butt (as goat).

sowanye, increase in strength.

sú, beat.

sú, roast.

sú, sing (kettle).

sú arụ, be fat.

sú ụzǫ, clean road.

sú ofụfụ, froth.

sụ nsụsụ, dodge, draw back something offered.

sụ ani, clear undergrowth.

sụ asụsụ ani, clean grass.

sụ ẹbwe, load gun.

sú ike n' ani, pay money to.

   ẹze of ebo, for death of ezubwo, (taking off his red
      cap).

sú ile, put out tongue (he is lying).

sụ' ima lima, speak foreign language.

sụ isi, knock head, tie cloth on head.

sụ isi n' ani, fall headlong.

sú nsụsụ, give and take back.

sụ ṅkpokolo imi, talk through nose.

sụ ǫifia, clean bush.

onye sụ nsụ, stammerer.

sú nsụsụ ani, clear grass.

sụ ude, groan.

sú, dip (bread in soup).

su ǫkalika, be vexed.

su ǫkịlịka, be vexed.

su ǫko, set on fire.

su ǫkpǫ, strike with hand (downwards).

sú nni ji, bristle (animal).

su ili, fight with co-respondent (Ala).

sụfie, pronounce wrong.

sugwo (ogwo), break in pieces.

sujie, die.

sụkbo asụsụ, speak language well.

sụkp̀e, mutter in sleep.

sukp̀ọ, burn up.

sule, burn.

suli-suli, very small, withered.

sulu, dip (yam) in oil.

sụniri, rise.

sụpe, break off piece of pestle.

sụpụ asụsụ, finish clearing bush.

susu (ọiyi), cause to quarrel.

susube iru, pretend anger.

susulu, taste.

sụta, cut grass for goat.

sụtu, knock down pole instead of hammering it into
    ground.

sụwẹ, break in pieces.

sụye, make small hole.

ši ạinya, look at person as if he were guilty.

šị (ri) ama, mask.

ši azu, move back.

ši', be transformed.

ši mili, leak.

šị (rị) ṅkp̀ụ, cry out.

šị oku, call.

šị šịnye (or rị rịnye), stick fast.

šị šẹdo, hold lightly.

šušubẹ, shake (liquid).


tá, bite, suffer, be dry, etc.—
    otal' àlo, he has bitten.

tá, dry.

tằ', be vexed.

ta ṅwoli ṅwoli, be vexed for nothing.

ta afofo, suffer.

ta' atằ, chew.

ta' ịtằ, win stake.

ta n̄kẹkẹle ẹze, grind teeth, masticate.

tá ụza, chew cud.

tá ẹgo, (O) play pitch and toss.

tá . . . n̄gige, stretch cord (across road.)

tằ, talk, tell story.

ta . . . awọ, reproach (by reminding of benefit).

ta ĩta, tell fable.

ta ịtasi, tell untruth.

ta ọ̀kọli, tell untruth.

tá ụǰala, chirp, cry (as child).

tá ụta, blame.

taba, fall (river).

taba nsi, try hard.

tabe, bite off.

tabe ainya, close eyes (disgust).

tabẹli, masticate (meat).

taboba, force to talk.

ọnụ atabobại, your mouth has run away with you.

tačali, (1) bite off, (2) gnaw.

tadide, stick.

tado, stop by coaxing, coax.

tado, adhere.

tagide, adhere tightly.

tagide ẹze, be patient.

tằinye n'ainya, prove, convict, declare.

tắiyali, chew round and round.

taǰili ataǰili, bite small (soft thing).

taka, tear with teeth.

takẹli, bite (hard thing).

takṗali, hide.

takwo, (pig) chew unripe corn, etc.

takwu ntakwu, whisper.

tali, persuade, take person by persuasion.

tàli, lead on, seduce.

tamagwẹle, girls' game.

tami, dry inside.

tamu, murmur.

tamu (ntamu), speak ill.

tanọ, coax.

tapụ, dry up.

tatu, throb (vein).

té, rub, dance, etc.

tê, to be far.

tẹ ẹgu, dance.

tẹ ẹte, smear.

tẹ́ nzu, rub chalk.

tẹ ofe, prepare soup.

tẹ, think.

tẽ, keep well.

tẽ, take person away (patient or criminal).

tẹ ńtîtê, be far

tẹbe ofe, make soup.

tẹkwasi, cook twice.

tẹkwẹbẹ, keep well, look after.

tẹlẹlẹ, smooth, level.

tẹli, abduct (child).

tẹlia, rub well.

tẹpu, expel (leper).

tẹpu nzu, rub out chalk.

tẹtẹ, recover (children).

tẹte ụla, wake up.

tẹtọ, make dirty.

tị́, àtị́, be extended.

tị̣ ẹrhi (O. O), be useless.

tí agogo, sound gong, bell.

tí, shine.

tí (aka), strike with hand.

ti ẹgwe, make wall (fence).

ti idẹbwe, have "friends" (married woman who leaves husband)

tí ikpa (On.), box (verb).

tí ọkpọ, box.

ti ńkụ, throw down wood (as suitor).

ti (oko) n'okute, strike against stone.

ti ogbolo, strike with staff.

ti ọkp̣ọ, strike horizontally.

tị̈, be famous ; be thick (soup).

tị̈, be spoiled ; disgrace.

   itịa, you have done a shameful thing.

tibẹ, break (cut) rope.

tibe (oiyi), cause to quarrel.

tịbue, beat to death.

tibwobo, break (pot, plate).

tičẹpu, brush.

tigwa, mix.

tigwẹli, strike back.

tiji, break (leg, arm).

tikọ ẹtiko, collide.

tịkp̣o arụ, get thin.

tinye aka na nni, dine.

tinye či, put in place of.

tínye kwu, add.

tinye . . . . n' okẹnu, promote.

tinye n' ọlụ, put to work.

tinye n' onọṅga, condemn, put in prison.

tinye okitikp̣a, be active.

tinye ọkụ, light.

tinye ọkụ n' ọko, put fire in pipe.

tinye ọnụ n' ofu, say same thing.

tinyụ, beat out.

tịpǔ, burst through.

tịpụ, stretch out.

tiputa okụ n' ọnụ, force (confession), etc.

tisa, break to pieces.

títo, be noised abroad.

titọsi, soil, make dirty.

tịtǔ, smite down, blow down.

tiwainye, put more.

tọ̌, loose, be unable to get out.

tǒ, praise.

tò, suit.

tọ, suffocate (kill)—
    iyi atọm n' afọ, iyi, oath kills me in my belly.
    ani atoi, may the ground kill you (when killing animal
      or to hinder witch from witchcraft).
tọ̈, spread.
tọ̈, place.
tọ̈ ainya, watch, expect.
tọ̀ atọ, remain.
tọ̀ nti, hearken.
tọ̈ ntọ ani, lay foundation.
tọ́ ntọmi, be last.
to (akbuji), big seed yams.
to eyu (A), become mouldy.
to mbwẹle, trade.
to nto, trick.
to ósè, swallow pepper wrong way.
tọbọ, put down (not load).
tọbọ ọgu, put medicine down.
tọbwọ (n'ani), put (one) down.
tọbwọ kpunčala, be desolate.
tọbwọ ṅkiti, lie down and do nothing; be desolate.
tọbwọ̈lo, put by itself.
tọbu, strangle.
tọdo, strangle, hold by throat (not kill).
toga ntoga, think much of oneself.
tojue, (flood) be at height.
tọke, break (chain), rip (seam).
tokọ ime, be pregnant (early stage).
tọkpọ, break egg by pecking.
tokwasi, hang (by cord).
tọkwasi (aka), put (hand) on.
tọlọ, peck.
tolotolo (O. A), soft.
tọpụ atọpu, get loose.
tosi—
    otosi ka mmẹ, to be under obligation to do.
tọtunẹte, slack, loose.

tọye, loose.

tsó', no.

tŭ, rain, pinch, mark.

tú, salute by title, suspect.

tŭ, shout.

tu, hunt, follow game.

tụ̀, throw—

  atụm, p.

  atoam, a.

  atobam, p. cont.

tụ̆, peck.

tụ̀, spatter, drop.

tu', stick in ground.

tụ (nnono), throw stone (at bird).

tu' afa, salute by title.

tú (atụ) agwa, be many coloured.

tụ́' akwa, strip.

tụ . . . asia, remind of gift (to reproach person).

tụ ebili, be agitated.

tụ ẹgu, fear.

tụ erhi, supply yams (husband; from iwaji till firing of
  new farm).

tú ẹtu (3rd p.), blister.

tụ iče, throw missile.

tu ikb̃ŏlo, put medicine to cause paralysis.

tụ̆ inu, speak proverb.

tụ́ ize, shudder.

tụ́ ji, dig yam to store.

tụ́ mainya, be drunk.

tụ mba, reprove.

tụ́ mbwẹle, trade.

tụ̆ mbọ, pinch with nail.

tụ́ nče, doubt.

tụ̆ ndu, breathe slowly.

tu ngugu, send present.

tu nkp̃o, husk kokonut.

tụ nkp̃ulụ, make raised beds for planting.

tụ̃ ntu, poke fun at.

tu ntutu, talk loud, reprove.

tụ̃ ntutu, differentiate.

tu nza, trick.

tụ obulubu, to be piled up.

tu' okpolo, run after and find.

tụ́ omimi, dive.

t̯ụ ona (O.A), shout at thief in market.

tu ọnụ, (nuts) begin to rot.

tụ̃ ọsọ, canter.

tụ́ ówụ̈, make thread.

tu ugo, put eagle feather in hair.

tụ ụkbŏlŏ, throw missiles.

tu ụ̣kpŏlŏ, follow tracks.

tụ ụla, make sleepy.

tụ́ ụla, entice by false pretences.

tụ ụla, slap.

tụ̃ ume, make arrangement.

t̯ụ ụnọ, build.

tụali, turn.

tụali mba, reprove.

tụba mbọ, fall in single drops.

tụba mbo, collect.

tụ̈ba obo, collect.

tụb̆ue, throw and kill ; bite and kill (?).

tub̆we ntubwe, work slowly.

tụča, peel.

tụča, bale canoe by shaking, hush by shaking.

tụča ntụča, be bold.

tụče, take bark off (roughly).

tụčẹ ntụčẹ, refuse to go alone.

tụdo, look for quarrel.

tudo, fasten.

tụfu, throw away.

tụfu n' obi, (Ub.) send wife to obi.

tụfu uče, forget; lose one's head.

tui, tui, yes, yes.

tụka n'ainya, astonish.

tụkali ọnụ, contradict one's superior.

tụkọ, throw together.

tukọ, regard, pay heed, trace.

tụkọnyesia, gather and throw in.

tukṗolu, be abundant.

tukwa, stoop.

tụkwasi, put upon ; throw again.

tụlụ, persuade.

tụlụ ndo, be paralysed.

tụlụ ume, arrange.

tụlụfọ, be a big heap.

tụlụfo, be unloaded (canoe), be deserted, left alone (farm).

tulu tulu, soft.

tuma, especially.

tụ ne ạtụne, hesitate.

tụni, be entangled.

tụnụ, be entangled.

tụnụdo, be entangled.

tụṅwa, become dry.

tụnye (O.O.), throw the shuttle.

tụnye, make collection.

tụnye (mili), drop (water).

tụnye alo (?), throw on.

tụnye n'im' ọko, throw into fire.

tụnye n' ụkwụ, come unexpectedly, be at hand.

tụra, throw down, throw person.

tụrapu, throw down.

tụte, wake ; make alive, revive.

tụtẹ ndo, revive.

tụtụ, pick up, pay (fee).

tụtụ, throw stones (at fruit).

tụtụba, collect.

tútụkọ, gather.

tụtụkọba (ṅkṗụlụ), collect (fruit).

tụwa ainya, see hidden things.

tụwụsa, drop on (rain).

ụbá, drum (burial).

ube (O.O), bent stick for snare.

ụbẽ (A), increase; thickly populated district.

ụbẹ, spear, throwing, with barbs (2 pronged fish spear, As.).

ụbé', plum tree; fruit of ube tree.

ụbẽ', end, limit.

ụbè (O), farm.

ụbé' (O), stature.

ubẹlẹte (Al.), chest for cloth.

ubẹṅko, barb (arrow) (spear).

ubı (Anam, On.), farm.

ubi, spitting cobra (crows like cock!).

ụbî (Ub.), " husband " of lo (= ajọmwọ́).

ubialǔ, stupid.

ubido, tiger cat.

ụbọ, vengeance.

ụbolo, brain.

ubolo, time.

ùbŏro, eggshell.

ubu, rotten (fish).

ụbụbwa, pot.

ubwlẹne (ọkoko), wing and tail feathers.

ubwiẹte, " mine "; lucky.

úbwŏ (O), farm.

ùbwŏ, hollow, (small) cave.

ubwoko, forest.

ùbwŏlŏ, walking stick.

ùbwŏlŏ ùbwŏlọ, often.

ubwome, dance waist ornament.

ubwonu, hole behind collar bone of sick or thin person.

ụbwụ́, net.

ụbwụ́, slip.

ùče, razor.

uda, tree sp. (spice).

ŭdẹ, resemblance (A. O).

ùdè, tree sp.

ùdè', top.

ùdẹ̀ olulu, spindle.

ůdě, nut oil.

udẹle (= ọ̀bwọ́), company.

udi, habits, way of doing things.

udomili (O. O), a kind of cloth.

ụ̀dụ́ (I. A), big water pot.

udu, guide—

    udu nẹdu ogoli nẹdu ọfumma, a man who conducts a woman should be a good guide.

udunni, cheap season.

ùfẻ, liar.

ufẹle (H), arrow.

ufẹle ằbani, wind (at night).

n' ufẹsi, across, over there (O, A).

úfiẻ, camwood.

ůfiẻ, drum.

n' ůfiẻ, across.

ufụge (On), crossbeam.

ùfỏ', speaking of absent person.

ufọdu, some.

ůfỏlỏ, ufỏi, empty.

ụ́fụ̀ (A), trouble, pain (mental), anger.

ùfù, tobacco.

ufu, hunger, famine.

ùfů, hole (store) in wall.

ùfů, "fox."

ụ̀gằ', (1) room, open space where people sit in house; also, (2) bush rope.

ugboko (uku), forest.

ůgẻ', dregs of palm wine.

ůgẻ, big "obulu."

ugẹbwe, (O) mirror.

ugẹge, end of palm leaf.

ụ̀gẹ̃lẻ, knife.

ữgẹ̀lẻ, watch tower.

ụgili, mango.

ugom (O), hill.

ůgů, hill.

ůgwů, circumcision; half; log.

ůyělě, yawning.

ůjà roar, bark.

ůjálá, chirp, crying loud.

uji, hole in tree.

uji, water, river (ŏlůlů = rises, ǫtita = falls).

uji aṅwu, rising of river without rain.

ůjů', multitude.

ujuju, leaf used for soup.

ojē ịkba ujuju = she has left her husband (she goes to
    fetch leaf).

ụka, conversation (A).

ukbo, mud seat.

ůkbŏ, hook (fish).

ụkbolo, hard mud.

ukbolo, missile.

ukęle, brave.

ůkǫ, messenger.

ůkŏ', cup.

ůkŏ', stand for drying fish.

ukokŏlo, green (" black ") palm nuts.

ukolo, snake sp.; ? Mamba.

ukolo azụ, eel (?).

ukommwa, spear trap.

ụkoti, hair " knife."

ůkpá, creeper with edible fruit (bitter after drinking water).

ůkpá, basket.

ukpętenyi, turtle.

ůkpŏ, barb, hook.

ůkpó, heap, seat.

ukpokpo, troublesome.

ukpŏlo (tu), ball.

ůkpŏgŏ, side of road.

úků ájá, first course of wall, level with ground.

ůků ji, leaf growth (yams).

úkwě, stump; tree left in farm.

ùḳwú', 50 cowries; bundle, inheritance, faggot (wood, yams) grass, 7 uku (at Okpanam), twopence.

ukwu olulu, skein of cotton.

ùḳwù, waist.

ùkwù ẹ̀zẹ̀, hollow in which teeth rest.

(ǰu) ukwẹle, enquiry.

ukwile, root of tongue.

ụ́ḳwụ́, foot.

ụ̀lá, slap.

ụ̀lánnọ̀, eight thousand.

ùlé, rotten (meat, yam).

ùlẹ̀, ofu ule, flat, same level.

ụlili, ground squirrel; *Euxerus erythropus.*

ulolo, gutter.

úlù, profit, luck.

ụ̀lụ̀, flesh, pulp.

ụ́lụ̀ anụ, meat.

ụ̀lụ̀ (O), mud.

ůlù, bottle.

ulubu, spear trap (falling spear).

ŭlukbu (mili), cloud.

ụluku ose, worthless person.

ulŭme, down (chicken).

uluru, unsuitable thing; (*e.g.*, if a man lies to each of two friends about the other).

ụmẹfu (O. O), red yam.

úmẹ̀ndọ̀, strong; pit of stomach.

umẹnẹkbọ, sweet.

umiakbo (O. O), red yam.

umuẹze (Al), one of two sections into which town is divided.

umuge (Ub.), young men.

umuma (I.A.), beater (for ground, grave, etc.).

umuwenne (Ezi), umunna.

ụnabwa (I.A.), boy's house.

ụnabwo, (Al.) house for childless old woman.

une, watchful eye, look out—

une kam nọdul'a, I am keeping an eye on him.

únẹ' (O), banana.

ůnẹ', musical bow.

ụnẹku, wife's house.

ụnọ', house.

ụnọ abwa, wood house.

ụnọ ičakwa (Ala), widow's house.

ụnọ igîlỹgî, house without door, used for walling up bad woman (e.g., isimwọ who ran).

ụnọ ikum, tower for ikum.

ụnọ nto widow's house.

ụnọ ụdụ, place for waterpot (in house).

ụnọ ofọ, leaf hut.

ụnọ ogidi (Og), widow's house.

ụnọ kokbo (O. O), bachelor's house.

ụnọnto (Okp.), widow's house (in Ogwashi ụnọnto is part of the woman's house).

ůnů, you.

ůnů, struggle, haste.

uṅwu, clean, white.

upẹte (Ezi), bead ornament.

uradî, basket for boiling palm nuts or filtering corn.

ůré', semen.

urẹko, way of doing things, habits.

úrhú', morning.

urhi (Ib.), going to husband's house at puberty.

urhu, incontinence of urine (woman).

uruči (I.A.), image of husband or dead wife; causes people to lose things if no fowl is offered; husband and wife eat.

uruči (Ezi), image of dead woman.

usẹku, kitchen, hearth for cooking.

ůsó, long—

ọbụruso, he is not long.

usŏlo, following precedent (?)

usuke, fruit, growing on shrub.

útẻ, bamboo stretcher (loom).

utỹli, stretching.

utolo, wall round king's house (Ogwaši, Isel' uku, etc.).

utǒlo, burial place for lepers.
utọmi, long life.
utukƀe, flat clay plate (Abọ, lamp).
utǔlu, yellow-backed duiker.
utǔlu, septum of nose.
utulukƀe, hawk sp.
ụwẹ, (Al.) world.
uyagami, injury.
ụ̌zụ̌ (A), noise (in town).
uzi (A), tree sp.
úzi, vapour, smoke.
ụzọ mmili mmili, very early.
ụ́zọ̌, door, road.
ụzọ nta, lane, cross-path.
ụzọ owẹle, lane, cross road, cross-path, path between neighbours' houses.

vé, jump off.
vio, (whip) crack, (heart) beat.

wạ̊, ache, tie cloth, put on.
wạ̊, boil, divide.
wá', they.
wá, cut, walk, etc.
wá', spread.
wá' ámu, be adult (*ca.* 18).
wá nǰapa, open (upwards).
wạ̊ (? 4), rush, burst, rise (sun).
wạ̊, smell good.
wạ, very nice (esp. of smell).
wá gwada gwada, walk slowly (purposely).
wá pọči pọči, walk slowly.
wá ǰi, eat new yams.
wá ṅgadaba, put out shoots.
wá (or wạ̊) nǰakƥa, split at joint.
wạ̊ ani, divide farms.
(isi) wå'(m), (head) ache.

wa afia, flatter.

wa ilǒ, make road.

wa ololo, make a gutter.

wači, stop leak (in roof).

wači ụnọ, keep the house (as idẹbwe).

wayalili, wander.

waiyale, wander.

walǎla (ụzọ, ụnọ, mili, ụ̇bwọ̇), narrow.

wápụta, burst out.

wasi aǰa, make balls of mud (for house).

wẹ bẹnẹte (ibu), lighten (load).

wẹ kwasi tata, till this day.

wẹbo ẹbibo, accuse.

wẹdata ani, humble.

wẹdẹtẹ, lower.

wẹdo, humiliate.

wẹfie ụgwọ, take for debt.

wẹku, rush at.

wẹlu nti toa n'ani, listen attentively.

wẹlǔe (na), till.

wẹluǰube, (moon) wax.

wẹluka n'osọ, take aside.

wẹni, rise (bread, etc.).

wẹni ụkwụ, walk fast.

wẹpu okp̣u, take off hat.

wẹpu uče, forget.

wẹputa, take out.

wẹruka (aka), take (hand) away.

wẹso . . . iwe, be annoyed with.

wẹte, bring (one thing).

wẹte (onye) ọfumma, receive well.

wẹwusa iwe, be angry with.

wọ, take fire—

ọko awọlo, the fuel is taking fire.

wọ, pick (mango).

wọ ada, stumble and recover.

wọ (awọ), put on, catch.

wǫ awǫ, do unintentionally.
wǫ awuwǫ (Al), be cunning.
wǫ ǫko, catch fire.
wǫ ǫnụ, ascertain from.
wó, buy (palm nuts).
wo' n'ainya, be clear.
woga, take fowl to market to sell.
wǫli, resemble parent.
wǫli, resemble.
wǫta, pick (fruit).
wǫta, understand.
wụ, at this time.
wụ', take out (with finger or tool).
wụ̈, do.
wụ̈, jump.
wụ̈ ṅwụwụ, jump.
wụ̈ ịkpǫtǫ, jump.
wụ̈ ṅtụ, jump.
wụ iwolo, cast skin.
wu', be famous—
    oku ęwugo, the matter is public.
wu', boil.
wu', wound.
wụ' ǫsǫ, run race.
wube, be famous.
wụbe ǫsǫ, start to run.
wụčǎputa, wash away.
wuči, stop, shut up.
wuči ụzǫ, declare road closed.
wụdǎ', jump down.
wudo, stand upright.
wụfe, jump over.
wuyepu, give leave for meeting.
wulu (object) stand ; (word) stand fast.
(ǫkụ) wulu, burn, light.
wụni, jump.
wụra (ęgo), put cowries on the ground.

wupu (iwu), abrogate (law).
wurafu ụkwụ, throw out feet in walking.
wurẹ, divide.
wụse, spill.
wụsi, put off (clothes).
wusie, throw down.
wụta, take out (with knife), etc.
wuwọ awuwọ, be loose, come loose.
wuye, revoke law.
wuyẹpu, give leave for meeting.


yá, barter, exchange.
yá uče, change one's mind.
yá, change colour.
yá ibu, change loads.
yá, he.
yá, throw.
yằ, be sick.
yá ẹgo, throw cowries (to dancers).
yẵ, pardon.
yằ', scatter (corn, beans).
yainye ẹgo, change money, throw money.
yại̯yali, wait.
yakọ, change together, mix.
yali, exchange.
yali, leave (behind).
yapu, exchange.
yasa mili, sprinkle water.
yẽ, cut.
yẽ, cook.
yẹ́ nti, listen.
yẹ́ ọnụ (m), defend, speak for—
    (yẹm ọnụ, answer).
yẹ́ oyẹ, be open.
yẹ́ uyẹle, yawn.

yệ˝, be together.

yệ̃ oiyị̆ (oiyim), be "friends."

yẹbẹ akwala, take off yam roots.

yeča (oku), lie.

yečẹfu, cut.

yẹde, cook too much.

akp̌ili yẹkọ, be thirsty.

yẹlẹ eyẹlẹ, be stupid.

yẹli eyẹli, have a hole.

yẹlu, be finished (Uk.).

yẹreye, be still uncooked.

yì, wear.

yi' (ntatalabụ), tickle.

yì, lay (egg).

yì, shout.

yì, put seed yam in hole.

yì, resemble.

yi ệyì, resemble.

yi, alone —
   sọ̀m yi', I alone.

yi aba, put "staple" in footstep (stops person).

yì egu, terrify.

yí ệyì, perish.

yî ìyì, lose, spoil —
   iyirigo, you have become worthless.

yi igwe (Al.), work together.

yi ọko, put out a fire (house burning).

yi ọko, fire (bush).

yi ǯkwukwọ̀, make difficulties, postpone.

yi oyi, turn somersault.

yi uče, think, suspect.

yifẹge, ferry.

yii ọkwŭkwọ, bale water from pool to catch fish.

yikp̌o, clothe.

yíọ̆, beg.

yiọ̆ (mba), challenge.

yitọ igwe, twist iron rods (two).

yiwa, cut open.

yọ̀! yọ̀! (shout at thief).

yọ (Al.), catch ball.

yọ́, beg.

yọ́, fall in pieces, decay.

yọ̀, collect cut grass.

yọ̀, strain.

yọ̀, sift

yọ̃, be cunning.

yọ ạiyiyọ, be cunning.

    me — (H.) be cunning.

yọ ada (Al.), stumble and recover.

yọ akọ, play knucklebones.

yọ mbwa, challenge to wrestle.

yọda ayọda, pull down, hang down side.

yọ́ko, collect in one place (grass, rope).

yọkọba (afifia), collect, gather.

yokoyoko, shining.

yọli, very soft.

yọta, get by begging.


zá, answer, support, meet.

zã̀, sweep.

    àzåm, I answer (or I sweep).

zå', answer.

zã̀, shine.

zå åzã̆, strain, get thin.

zá åzå, swell.

za izu, go to eat in house of ẹze at feast.

zạči, close.

zagide, fasten, put firm, a prop.

zam zam, not at all.

zata mili, get clean water.

zẹ̀, shun, beware of.

zẹ ndu, avoid . . . so as to live.

zè (ṅdọ̀), shelter.

zĕ, get good breeding goat.

zẹ́, tell.

ze', slip down (wall).

zĕ anụ, follow game.

zĕ anu ẹ̀zĕ, creep quietly after animal.

zĕ ọ́dụ̀, make yam shelter (farm).

zĕ ọkụ, be hot.

zẹkwaba, keep well.

zẹli mili, shelter from rain.

zi, be straight.

ži, stand, be open (market).

zí, please with work.

zì, send.

z ì, tell.

zì nlo, tell dream.

zì aka, point.

zi ṅwŭlu, burn.

zí ẹ̀zǐ, send.

zì ozi, send messenger.

zì ẹ̆zì, borrow.

zì ibu, put down load.

zì imi, blow nose.

zide, go down (swelling).

zide, descend.

zido (ibu), put down load.

zige onye ozi, send messenger.

zìnạba, send home.

zipụ, send out.

zisa, proclaim.

zìta, borrow.

zize (wick) burn away.

zize ọnụ, mock someone.

zizipu, (Uk.) shake up.

zọ (ṅwunye), strive for same woman as wife

zọ̀, forget.

zọ́ ọzizọ, tread mud.

zó, tie.

zo ozizo, tie knot.

(aka) zó, point at.

zọ, mash (with foot).

zọ̃, care for, get good breeding goat.

zọ́, remember, cure.

zọ̃, train.

zọ́ afia, trade.

zọbu, tread to death.

zọbu (ji), destroy in farm.

zọdo, tread; keep back.

zọji, break with foot (wood).

zoko, join.

zọkpọ́, break with foot (egg or fragile thing).

zọkwasi, tread on.

zokwudo, join.

zolu (intrs.), shelter, be hidden.

zọputa, heal, save.

zọtọ, tread in dirt.

zọwa, break (glass).

zụ, tread mud.

zụ́ okwe, play mancala.

zụ́ ụ̀zụ̀, make noise.

zu, be content.

zũ, meet, suffice for.

zú (ori), steal.

zũ ike, rest.

zũ oke, fulfil; complete.

zùbě, consider what to do.

zụbu afia, cheat by giving too little money.

zụlụ nzụlụ, mutter, "growl" in sleep, grumble.

(okporo) zụpụ afia, unsuccessful trader.

zusa, alter plan.

zuzu (1) arrange, plan, (2) rub.

zuzu nzuzu, make foolish, act foolishly.

# ADDENDA AND CORRIGENDA
# TO IBO REPORT, PART II.

# ADDENDA AND CORRIGENDA TO IBO REPORT, PART II.

110. For abŏzǫ, cross roads, read abῠzǫ.
    To ạbŭba, down, feathers, add (wing and tail).
111. For ạbwáìgwe (O), cloud, read ạbwá ịgwe.
    To ἄbwadi, measure, etc., add *i.e.*, 5s.
    5th line from end read agam abwata ǫzǫ.
112. áči, tree, for carried read bent, after also add as.
113. For afịfya, grass, read afịfia.
    For afiǫmǫ ǫbula, roller, read afiǫmǫ ǫbala.
114. For afofo, labour, read ἄfụfụ.
    For ạgá', needle, read ạ̈gá'.
115. To àgᾰla (kpa), etc., add and partially burnt.
    For agaṅgwu, crocodile, read agaṅwu.
116. To agŏlo (A), plant, add used in medicine.
    To Ăgòlò, town, add of Agolo.
    To águgǫ̀, prisoner, etc., add denial.
117. To aɣala, wastrel, etc., add confusion, noise.
    ayịtu (O) for night fishing read stream and for fish,
        read stream.
    Delete àgᾰlu (A), bush cat.
    ạinya atǫlo, for blue (eyes, sheep) read blue eyes
        (sheep).
    For ạinya ǫgǫle (O), hazel eyes, read ạinya ǫɣǫle.
118. ạinyaṅwʼu ače potǫza, for ače read ači.
    To ajáru, ill luck, add sickness.
120. For ạ̈jo, headpad, read ạ̈jụ.
    To aká nine add (A).
    For aká ntagide read aká ntadide.
    akakbǫ̀ (A), thickset and short, delete (A).

121.  akakbọ̀ (ọka) (A), to last year's add (corn).
      For akaláka (O), cup, read akalăka or alalăka.
      To akalolia, hand, etc., add malformation.
      To akanzo, finger disease, etc., add whitlow.

122.  For akávo (O), last year, read akăvo.
      For akbạ̀ká (A), bag, read akƁăká.
      For akƁàkƁwa (O), top, read akƁăkƁwa.
      To akƁakŭlu, bowel (large), add stomach.

123.  To akƁata (ọnu) (O), story, add proverb.

124.  For akƁokƁŏko (O), boot, sandal, read akƁokƁŏko.
      For akƁokƁŏkṗa (A), boot, sandal, read akƁo-
          kƁŏkṗa.
      For akẹ̆kà, ant, white, read akị̀ka.

125.  akomilị́gwe (O), for nut-sky-water read nut-water-
      sky.

126.  àḳú, palm leaf, for weaker read weather.
      For ắkuḳwọ, book, read ắḳwuḳwọ.
      For akukwọ̆ndò, green, read akwukwọ̆ndò.

127.  For aḳwụ́ (O), palm leaf, read aḳwụ́.

128.  For alagolo, dirt, read alogolo.
      For alaniozọka read alamozọka.

129.  After alọ ji read alụ ji (A), yam.
      11th line from end, for ọ̀kwọ̀ read ọ̀kwờ.
      To amafia, toothache, add (also eye or ear).

130.  2nd line from top, for obọ̀ read obwọ̀.
      To amamife (A), sensible man, add knowledge.
      For amu, penis, read amụ, testicle; in example, for
          penis read testicle.
      For amu, penis, read amuda, house slave.

131.  To amwofolo, etc., add one who has lost testicles.
      8th line from top, for ňočĭčĭ read nụčĭčĭ.
      For anabwagăli (A), read anabwayăli.
      To ạnì (O), earth, add measuring, low, land, con-
          tempt.

132.  12th line from top, for èṅwĕelừm read èṅwĕlừm.
      To aṅwulu (A), soot, add smoke.
      To aṅanri, etc., add stink ant.

133.  To ărimwa, signal, add mark.
135.  12th line from top, for ò bĭdŏ read ò bodŏ.
136.  For ato (atokụ) read atò (atoḳwụ).
      For avụyụ (A), cricket, read avụzụ.
137.  5th line from top, for panel read frame.
      To awọ, stomach add Nibo.
      awọ̀ di nbala, for in bush read (bush).
      To awọ̀lọ̀ (agwọ), etc., add mask.
      To azi (O), child, add present generation.
      For ẹjẹ̃zina, ẹ̃jẹna read ẹjẹ̃zina.
138.  Under ăzŏ', back, for åzŏzå read åzŏyå.
      Under ăzụzụ, catarrh, in azụzụ (e), me, delete comma.
      Last line read obata n'onọ, he enters the house (by
        person standing inside).
139.  3rd line, for ọbarọẹlẹle read ọbarọ ẹlẹle.
      4th line from top add, make profit.
      To (a)ba mba, etc., add rebuke.
      Under (a)ba ulu, for ọbarọulu read ọbarọ ulu.
      To (a)bača, etc., add wash out.
      For (a)bakwu read (a)bwakwu.
      For (e)bẹ (A), cry, read (e)bé.
      Under (e)bẹ, cry, for bemiye read benniye.
140.  For (e)be, nearly, read be.
      For (e)bẹ̀, *go*, read (e)be *go*.
      3rd line from top add string.
      4th line, for ọbẹ̀ lelili read ọbẹ̀l' elili.
      For (e)bẹ *lu* ngu read (e)bẹ *lu* ugu.
      For obẹ ngu read obẹ ugu.
      (e)bebe *lu*, after lean insert (act.)
      Last line add cut.
141.  4th line, for inebenenni read inebene nni.
      For (e)bẹṅkpilipi read (e)bẹṅkpilikpi.
      For (e)bẹpugo read (e)bẹpu.
      Under (a)bia *lu*, for obiangŏ read ọbianagŏ.
      Under (a)bia *lu* oná, for abiaromoná read
        abiarọm oná.
      Last line add press, restrain.

142.  For bikọ, dwell together, read (e)bikọ.
      bịlibịliči, delete and evening.
      3rd line from end, delete abọlum.

143.  (a)bonyụa, for water, read with water from mouth.
      5th line from end, add make large.
      Under (e)bu *lu*, make large, insert obulu îbú, it's:
          (too) big.

144.  2nd line from top, read ubwọ nuwa abul' ibu.
      3rd line from top, for it's too big read he carries a load.
      For (e)bu ozọ read (e)bu ụzọ.
      To.(e)bučasi (a), etc., add be big enough (As.).

145.  5th line from top, for ekẹka read akẹka.
      For (e)bue aińya read (e)bue ainya.

146.  To ebulu ụzọ, etc., add be in front.
      Indented under (e)bupu, delete ?
      For bwa (O), dark, read (a)bwa', be dark.

147.  Under abwǎ' (A), scrape, for adwanainya read
          abwanainya.
      To (e)bwǎ, bind broken limb, add put splint.
      For (â)bwa, buy, read (a)bwa.
      To (a)bwá', make war, shoot, add fire, pour (water).

148.  5th line from top, read ọbwalo aka ana.
      To (a)bwá' ama, etc., add bear witness.
      Under (a)bwǎ ặrọ̀, for ogobwaro ặrọ̀ read
          ogagbwarọ, delete ặrọ̀.
      (a)bwa bebe, for (trans.) read (intrans.).
      For (a)bwa bulu, run past, before (shoot and kill)
          read (a)bwabulu, run past, before (shoot and kill).
      To (a)bwa ẹgo', etc., add count.
      Under (a)bwa ikbẹle, for nneyaala raed nneya
          ala.
      For (a)bwa ngọ̀ńgọ read (a)bwa ńgọ̀ńgọ.

149.  For (e)bwa nta read (a)bwa nta.
      To (a)bwa ðbọsi, fix (day), add name days on which
          things were done.
      After (e)bwa onọ, run home, insert (a)bwa ụnọ
          burn house.

(a)bwa *lu* ǫtǫ (A), be naked, delete (A) and add loose cloth.

(a)bwa *lu* ǫ̀tǫ, be naked, for be naked, etc. read tread clay for building.

To (a)bwa ume, etc., add comfort.

For (e)bwabu, shoot, read scramble.

To (a)bwabu ókụ, etc., add jumble words.

To (a)bwači bodo, etc., add foil.

(a)bwačiya, for law read land, delete brackets.

For (a)bwačula, read (a)bwačieta for law read land.

150.  To (a)bwado, stick in throat, add stick (arrow); hold by throat.

For (a)bwado *lu*, reckon read (a)bwadŏlu.

For (a)bwado *lu* (O), sulk, read (a)bwadŏlu.

4th and 5th line from top, delete brackets.

To (a)bwafie, etc., add miss.

(a)bwagǫ̆lǫ bwag ǫ̆lǫ, lean (be bent), delete brackets.

Under (a)bwagolo, read òsisi ǫbwagolo‚bwagolo.

For (a)bwagu read (a)bwa *gu*.

151.  To (a)bwámbǫ̀, etc., add persist.

To (a)bwanari *li*, run past, add outrun.

(a)bwanwuba iru, delete photograph.

3rd line from end add run away.

Last line add descend.

152.  (e)bwatie okwo, delete okwo.

To (a)bwazie *li*, explain, add make straight.

(a)bwǫ *lu*, bark, after (a)bwǫ insert (uja).

153.  (e)bwodo, for staunch read stanch.

For abwǫka *lu* read (a)bwǫka *lu*.

8th line from end add I do not know (how), it surprises me.

Delete 6th and 7th lines from end.

3rd line from end delete to.

154.  For (e) čǫlu uče read (e) če *lu* uče.

155.  To (a)čiča, loot, etc., add rub off.

(e)čičie, rub, after wood insert comma, and (put wood where people want to sit) delete brackets.

For (a)čie read (e)čie.

156. (e)čipu (O), go away, add untwist.

For (e)čįta, collect a few, read (a)čįta.

To acǫ *lu* oķu, etc., add provoke.

157. To (a) čụ *lu*, drive, add hunt.

To (e)ču ęču, (A), fail, add be half finished.

To (e)čue *lu* add (iyi).

To (e)čue iči add greedy.

(a)cuciya *lu*, after flight, insert semi-colon and delete brackets.

(e)čuleču, for be half changed read changed.

To (a)då *lu*, fall, add happen, befall.

158. (a)då *lu* (O), pain, delete (unipers).

2nd line from top, for ifanadam read if'anadam.

To (a)da ndamainya, etc., add imitate.

5th line from end, delete brackets.

159. To (a)dakwulu, etc., add get caught on.

For (a)dapwia read (a)dapia.

After (a)data insert (a)dawa, fall and break, and (a)daware, fall and break.

Under (e)de; rumble, to, mili nèdé, etc., add rain rumbles.

To (e)de *lu*, wet (trans.), add be wet.

Delete last line.

160. To (e)dębę *lu*, keep preserve, add appoint.

To (e)dępu *lu*, finish writing, add cancel.

3rd line from end read adim ndodin'enu àkwàm.

161. For (a)di nču read (a)di uču.

For (a)di ǫbe, be difficult, read (a)diǫ ụ.

For di ękę lęsu read di ękęlęsu.

162. For di ogoli ṅwaiyi, woman who make palaver, etc. read di ogoli ṅwainye.

For di nču read di uču.

For dibya read dĭbia.

Indented under (e)dĭbęlu, for vegweya read vegwiya, and after better insert (it is less a little).

163. 1st line read (big) farmer.

Under dika, delete dikatata.

To dike, by force, add strong person.

Indented under (a)dili ndo', for aru dili nnu read arụ dili unu, and add are you well.

To adilim ndo add I am alive.

For (a)dinyeli go *lu* read (a)dinyeli *go lu.*

164. For (e)do lu nisi read (e)do *lu* nisi.

To (e)do òdidò, etc., add aim.

165. For (e)docie ainye ife read (e)docie ainya ife.

To (a)doyalie, etc., add re-arrange.

(a)dọinye obwa, for basket read calabash.

(a)doka nninni, for lower (price) read be stubborn.

For (a)dolo nisi read (a)dolu nisi.

For (a)dọnia adọni read (a)dọni adọni

166. For (a)dowaga iru read (e)dowaga iru and after face add be given to.

To (e)dozie, put right add repair, prepare.

167. To ụ̃bẹ́nẹ́bé, somersault, add catherine wheel.

To ẹbo, town, etc., add quarter.

168. To ẹbúbú, (O) marks add (A. neck or arm).

To ẹbunụkụ, etc., add calf.

For ébwa ígono read ébwa ígono.

169. For ebwaoyọ read ebwa oyọ.

170. To ẹ́bwǎtiaka, etc., add cracking fingers.

For ẹbwẹli aǰa read ẹbwẹle aǰa.

For ẹbwẹn' ụbosi read ẹbwẹ n'ụbọsi.

After eǔiakbonwanneǔi, etc., add (two days after to-morrow).

To ecidinọfo, etc., add (let to-morrow be so).

171. Delete line 5.

172. For ẹgẹdege, (O), standing on tiptoe read ẹgẹnege

173. For ẹgọsabainya read ẹgọ̃galainya.

ẹgú (A), stick for hoe, delete (A).

To eǰiǰi, etc., add dress.

174. Under éka, place, for where am I going ? read where
    are you going ? and for eka onye nata gali read
    eka onye nata ɣali.
    For ẹkati read ẹkanti.
    ẹkƀa, fish, for fish read fist.

175. ẹkẹtẹ, for way read wax.

176. To ẹkulo, bird species, add (greater plantain eater).
    ẹ́lẹ́ obwẹne, for antennae read cock's comb.
    ẹle ɔkba, for antennae read cock's comb.

177. For ẹlo agada read ẹlo (agada).

178. To enyò (A), mirror, add telescope.

179. Under ẹtĩti, middle, for ọ̀dè read ọ̀dị̀.

180. To étu, like, as, add so.
    For ẹvùlévu read ẹvùlévu.

181. To ezenkwaba, etc., add supernumerary teeth.
    Last line, for òbù read òbụ̀.

182. Delete last line but one.
    Last line add Agolo.

183. Before fá', they, insert fá', now.
    2nd line, add stuff.
    3rd line, add stuff, squeeze.
    To (e)fe' mili, etc., add sprinkle water.
    (e)fejie *li* aka, for shake-hand read shake hand.

184. 1st line, add support, make fire proof.
    To (e)fiali, etc., add turn.
    Under (e)fibe (afa), for efibem afia read (e)fibe afia,
    and for efibem ẹgu read (e)fibe ẹgu.
    To (e)fibe (akukwa), put out supports, add (for
    pots).
    To (e)fie miss (aim) add err, do wrong.
    (e)fiẹpu, dislocate (arm) fall down, for fall down read
    by falling down.
    To (a)fiko, etc., add wring.
    To (e)fime, etc., add be in doubt.

185. Under (e)fobe, dawn, to—
    či ẹfobe, etc., add 6.0 a.m.
    či ejibe, etc., add darkness is coming (?)

či fonata, etc., add 6.30 a.m.

či eǰiribegwe, etc., add 6.0 p.m.

či erunętevegwe, etc., add 4.0 p.m.

či eǰirigo, etc., add 8.0 p.m.

(a)foča *lu*, for " seize," " finish " read stop seizing.

To (a)fǫdu, etc., add be left over.

186. Under (a)fy̨', see, and after ainya adafŏńti, insert ǫfy̨ ofu anadačǫ, he sees something he does not want.

To (a)fy̨ (O), pinch add hurt.

To (a)fy̨ča, blow, add winnow, see clearly.

To (a)fy̨čata *lu*, look well and find, add see point.

187. Under (e)fulu, suit bracket, ǫfy̨lu kam, he sees me much.

For (a)fy̨t'ąli read (a)fy̨tąli.

188. For ga (A), go, read ga, go (sign of future) and indented under ga, for gaiǰe read gęǰe.

4th line read go (take).

To (a)gaba, etc., add forward.

To gana gana (O), shaking, add walking slowly.

For (a)gbawusi read (a)bwawusi.

For gbęle gbęle read b̌węle b̌węle.

189. For gbwakanti read bwakânti.

Under ge, not, for ot age, read otage.

For (e) go, count read (a) gǫ.

190. Under ágo' (n)agu, for ago golum read agogolum.

To (a)goa *gu* esa, chatter, add curse.

Under (a)gǫdo, keep, for ag ǫdolum read agǫdolum

For (a)gopoto *lu* read (a)gopota *lu* and add count out.

191. Indented under (a)gu *lu*, finish, delete o'bučasia, he kills (finish).

To (e)gu ègú, (O), play, add dance.

For (a)gu *bu* mili (n)agy̨ read agy̨ mili (n)agy̨.

(a)gu ora, for be red hot read be (red) hot.

192. For (e)gupue read (e)gwupue.

For (e)guputa read (e)gwuputa and delete bǫputa ji dig up yams that have no roots.

(a)gwa', tell, after (a)gwa' add ǫgwa.

To (a)gwaba, mix, add tell.

For (e)gwe ini read (e)gue ini.

To (a)gwǫ' (O), cure, add make medicine.

Under (a)gwǫ', cure for otolo read oṭolo.

193. (a)gwǫ' ala, for be beaten too much read beat too much.

To (a) yạ̀ lu, stop, add turn back.

To (a)ya' lu ainya, look back, add and turn the eyes.

To (a)ya lu uče, convince, add change mind.

Under (a) yalialu, wait, for. ayalialĭmù read ayalialŭmì, and for ăgǎlialimu read ằyǎlialumì.

Indented under (a) yalu, leave alone, for ayanene read oyanene.

194. For (e)yẹ ugẹle, yawn, read (e)yẹ́ uyẹle.

ibaba, for sandfly read insect.

Under ibẹ, household, for bŭíbệm read bŭ í bệm.

195. To ibe, piece, bit (wide) add " shares."

4th line from end, for plant read plank, and add quarter of kola (ibè ǫ̌ji).

196. Under ibu, load, for ǫbŏnŭkŭ read ǫbŭ́ nŭkŭ.

For ịbwi (O), gums, read ịbwi.

197. To íčekù, charcoal, add tamarind tree.

Under ičẹóku, for íčẹokụ̆m read íčŏkụ̂m.

For indandamaìnya read indandamainya.

For ịdarai read ịdaru.

198. To ịdịm ụkwụ, etc. add foot.

For ịdu ǫdò read ịdǫ ǫdǫ.

199. ífẹ̀', thing, delete (A), add anything; and insert a iny; adakpǫzi ǫgo mwad'ili ife, we don't call 200 men anything.

200. For ígŏgo eyuna read ígŏgụ eyuna.

202. To ĭkòkbò (O), person always vexed, fussy person, add one who makes much noise and does little.

203. 2nd line, for ǫrilike read ǫsilike.

To ike, buttocks, add anus.

For ikẹ́wǫ read ikẹ́kwǫ.

204. For ikwộtọ read ikwộtọ.
205. For ịlinịsi, sixteen read ilinìsi.
206. For ìnéke, are you ready, read ìnǧke.
     For ịnĩozù read ịnìozù.
207. 3rd line, for terms read term.
208. Delete ir'nọkò, being hot.
209. ịsiạihia, read one million six hundred thousand and add
     (Oweri language).
     For isiànọ̀ read isiụnọ̀.
210. For ìsìnwạiyè read ìsìnwạinyè.
     After itẹgẹte, nine, insert itẹko, breaking pot on
     fire.
211. For ituadò read ịtualò.
     For ịtùkb̀ò read ịtũkbò, and add blistering.
     To ivejiọ́ko (O), yam, add magic for yams (or alose).
     For ivilĩvi (O), round thing, read ivilĩvi.
213. Under ìzù (A), meeting, for amwag' ife read amwar
     ife.
214. Under (e)ǰali, walk about, for quarter read town.
     (e)ǰẹbe, go past read go (past).
     For (e)jẹbẹ n'obọ read (e)jẹbẹ n'obwọ.
     3rd line from end, for *fragrante* read *flagrante*.
215. Under (e)ǰerube *lu*, for quarter read town.
     Indented uuder (e)ǰi, take, for fagejịjẹ read fagejịjẹ.
     For (a)ǰi iwe read (e)ǰi iwe.
     For (a)ǰi ọ̌ji read (e) ǰi ọ̌ji.
     Under (e)ǰide, hold, after sobers add me.
     To (e)ǰie ibo, fall down, etc., add (sand into water).
     For (e)ǰie ofu ọnu, read (e) ǰi ofu ọnụ.
216. 1st line, for (e)ǰieọpọ read (e)ǰi ọfọ.
     To (e)ǰikwa *lu*, hold in hand, add and break.
     Under (e)ǰimi, be far advanced, for is far night, read
     night is far, and add 12 p.m.
     7th line from end, after (a) jụlụ, insert (ajụ).
217. End line add be cold.
     (a) junata agu mili, for *e.g.* read *i.e.* and delete
     añoam, I drink.

Under (a)ǰuputá', for ọ ǰuputá' read ọǰuputá'.

Under ka, past, for okagurie read okazurie.

218.   To (a)ka, draw line, add mark, appoint.

To (a)ká arụ, be strong, add fearless.

Under (a)ka *gu* nka, for ọka *gu* read ọka gu.

For(a) kạba utewụ read (a)kạba ụ̣kwụ.

Delete akala, line.

For kama, better, read kamwa, and under kama for okạma read okạmwa.

219.   2nd line from end, for (a)kƀa *lu* akƀa read (a)kƀa *lu* ụkƀa.

Last line, for nakbakpa read nakbụkṗa.

220.   4th line from top, bracket female for sake of breeding.

For (a)kƀa (m)mba read (a)kƀa mba.

For (a)kƀa ṅwa nuka read (a)k̇ƀa ṅwa n'aka.

(a)kba *lu* oke, after peg insert comma instead of —, and indented under (a)kba *lu* oke, after boundary add or separate.

For (a)kƀa ọnụ ifé, plait mouth of bag read (a)kƀa ọnụ ife.

221.   For (a)kƀafie (ozọ), lose way, read (a)bwafie (ụzọ).

For (a)kƀafụe *lu*, be lost, read (a)bwafụe *lu*.

(a)kƀaye, for tick read teeth.

(a)kbaǰie, for cut (kola, corn) read (kola, corn), cut.

For (a)kƀakasi read (a)bwakasi.

For (a)kbàkọ *lu* read (a)bwakọ.

For (a)kbakọta read (a)bwakọta.

(a)kƀapu, take off, after go away add for walk.

Indented under (a)kbaputa, retract, for ọna akbaputalia okú nọnu read ọnakbaputalia okụ́ n'ọnụ.

For (a) kƀasili (ozọ) show (way) read (a) bwazilî (ụzọ).

222.   For (a)kbatoa, shout, read (a)kbotoa.

(e)kƀe *lu*, judge, after (e)kƀe add ikƀe.

To (e)kbebue, win case add report against.

For (a)kḅọ aka, throw in, read kḅọ aka.

223.  To (a)kḅọ *lu* ọ́ko, burn, add set fire to.

For (ẹ)kbo . . . ukḅo kill, read kḅo. . úkḅó.

(a)kḅoa i̯gwe načača, for cold, read hot and for (a)kboa read kḅoa.

(a)kḅoa *lu* n'ani, etc., add creep on ground.

To (a)kḅočie, shut, add lock.

Under (e)kḅue *lu*, for iǰi (e)kpolu read iǰi (e)kḅolu.

224.  Under (e)kbučie ọnụ delete banọnkẹte, keep silence.

225.  Line 2, add dress.

(e)kekwa, read mend (roof).

226.  Delete 1st line.

For (a)kimwo *lu*, replant, read (a)kuṅwo *lu*.

For (a)kụ́ *lu*, scrape, read (a)kó àkọ̀ *lu*.

For (a)ko, collect, read (a)kọ, collect.

3rd line from end, for kànkọ read känkọ.

Last line, add creep.

227.  5th line, for nko read uko.

To (a)kọ *lu* ọkọ̀, scratch, add itch.

For (e)kọ ọnuma read (e)ko ọnuma.

For (a)koam i̯gono read (a)koa i̯gono.

To (e)koe *lu*, be strong, add ready.

For (a)kolia read (a)kalia.

228.  For koni kom read koṅ kom.

For (a)kpa amu, play, read kṗa amu.

For (a)kpa *lu* amu, cause to laugh, read kṗa amu.

To (a)kṗaba, mould (in earth), add begin to dress hair.

Indented under (a)kṗabo (O), close up, for ogaineriọtọ read oganeriọtọ, and for not, read it stands up.

To (a)kṗainya isi, etc., add comb dressed hair or rub oil.

3rd line from end add get.

229. Under (a)kp̣ọ, call, insert, ọkpọbia n' ụnọ, he calls
him in, and ọkpọbalia, he calls him in.

To (akbẹli) (a) kp̣ọ ńko (A), be thirsty, add dry.

Indented under (a)kp̣ọ ọ́ko, be hot, for iruakp̣ọ(m)
read iru akp̣ọ(m).

Delete example under (a)kp̣ọdo, plant peg.

For (e)kpọkọbe read (e)kpokọba.

kp̣okp̣alàla, for holding tight, thing (long and
slender) thing, read holding tight long and slender
thing.

For (a)kp̣ọle le, burn, read (a)kpọle li.

For (a)kp̣ọle le, roll along, read (a)kpọle li.

8th line from end, for akpọlenyem read akpọlenye.

230. For (e)kp̣upu ókpu read (e)kp̣ubu ókpu.

To (e)kuča ola, snore, add sleep.

For (e)kudide read (e)kwudide and add stand still.

For (a)kudo (A), meet, read (e)kudo.

231. 4th line from top, add hold child by hand, in arms.

For (a)kufie ọno read (a)kwufie ọnụ.

For kulọtọ read kwulọtọ.

For (a)kulu gu ẹkẹlesu read (a)kwụlụ gu ẹkẹlesu.

232. For (a)kusi nebe read (a)kwụsi n'ebe.

For (a)kusi ọlụ read (a)kwụsi ọlụ.

To (a)kwa ọnụ, refuse obedience (habitually), add
deny.

233. To (a)kwačiɣa lu, etc., add carry back.

(a)kwalu ife, go home, after ife insert na.

Under (a)kwana, enter, for eǰe akwanago nara read
iǰe akwanago n'arụ.

To (a)kwanaba lu ife, go home (of wife), add carry
things.

234. For (e)kwẹkọ, tie securely, read (e)kwẹkọ.

To (a)kwọ̌', ride, add carry on back.

Under (a)kwọ̌', ride, for cow read witch, for witch read
cow, and for rides read carries him.

4th line from end, add miscarry.

Last line, for (a)kwoga read (a)kwụga.

235. 2nd line, for smooth, (skin) level, read smooth (skin), level.

To (a)kwǫta, etc., add bring.

Under (e)kwu, stand and stare, for skeleton read masker.

Delete 3rd line from end.

236. (a)kwusi, for wait for read wait.

To (a)lá', drink add eat (as moth).

For (a)la(ola) ago, read (a)la (ųla) ago.

For (a)lanwą̊go read (a)la ṅwago.

For (a)labandi read (a)laba di.

To (a)lace *lu*, lick, add eat juicy fruit.

To (a)lado etc., add be fixed.

237. For (a)lamdi read (a)la di.

For (e)le *go*, burn, read (e)lę (ǫko) *go*.

For (e)lę *lu* ule, rot, read (e)lę́ *lu* ule, and add be rotten, lazy, greedy.

238. (a)lia *go*, for climb read creep (insects).

(e)libido, for leave read stay.

5th line from end delete brackets.

239. For (e)lifę̣li (uli), climb across, read (a)lịfę̣li (uli).

For (a)lo aniya read (a)lǫ ainya, and add contemptuously.

240. 4th line, add do evil.

To (a)lokḃue etc. add miscount.

To (a)lǫkwa aka etc. add break.

241. under (e)lu *lu*, reach, insert mili elue, the river is full ; rain is coming.

indent ainyamelurǫ, and for you read it.

Delete jim nese nenyę̣m, I grow yams, indented

(e)lu, grow. (e)lu gu ogo, etc., for reach old age, be old, read grow big.

For (a)lua, put small stick, etc., read (a)lǫ́a.

For (a)lua *lu* aro, read (e)lue *lu* arų.

For (e)lubue, peg animal down till it dies, read (a)luḃue, and add not understand what a blacksmith is making.

242.    3rd line, add overflow, hover (bird).

To (a)lu̱tu̱, touch with one finger, add prick.

242–243.    For ma read mwa.

To (a)majie, etc., add fold double.

To mwaka (O), because, add concerning, whether, however.

For (a)maula, read (a)ma ula.

244.    For m̀baǰa read m̀bwaǰa.

To mbala, compound, court, add large room.

For m̀banozo read mbanu̱zo̱.

For mbara read m̀barà.

250.    To mbwằko̱, joining together, add seam.

For mbalou̱nsi read mbalónsi.

251.    For m̀bwe ba bwara read m̀bwe fa bwava.

253.    Under (e)mę ebęle, insert ębęlei męlum, I am sorry for you.

For (e)mebie (koṅwe) o̱ičá read (e)mebe (koṅwe) o̱ičá, and delete (?)

Indented under (e)mečie *lu*, close, for emečilum o̱no read emecilim o̱noi.

For (e)megoto read (e)megote.

2nd line from end add do together.

254.    3rd line from top for (a)meli̱ read (a)meli.

For (a)melie, powder, read (a)melia.

Under mêmé, red, for îrûm nênwûu m̀èèmè read îrûm nênwû mềmề.

For (a)menyu̱a *lu* o̱ko read (e)menyu̱a *lu* o̱ko.

Eor (a)mepua *lu* read (a)mi̱pua *lu*.

To (e)męsue, be finished, add finish.

For (e)męsie *lu* read (e)mesie *lu*.

For (a)meta *lu*, pull out, etc,, read (a)mi̱ta *lu*

255.    For m̀fidò, pressing, read m̀fidò.

To mfifie, shaking head, add hand.

256.    To (e)mie o̱nu̱, pout, add be envious.

For mikalo (O), lizard, read (o)mikalo.

To mili gologolo, etc., add water dripping into pot.

Under mmá, mwa, good, for anam ǫ̈fuma read
anǫm ǫ̈fuma.

257.  ṁmìmì read disease (? tuberculosis of bone).

258.  For (a)moa *lu* ndęne read (a)mųa *lu* udęne.
For mòmá read mòmwá.
Under mpo, big man, insert mę mpo, act as big man
(in dance).
To ṁpoto, koko, etc., add cooked with red yam.
Indented under (a)mų, light, for nue read nne.

260.  Indented under (a)mwa, hold, delete brackets and add
homesickness.
2nd line from end add sniff.

261.  For (a)mwa *lu* ǫlá read (a)mwa' *lu* ola.

262.  (a)mwakwuba for cow read cord, and add˙ catch
hold of.
For (a)mwalu, beat, read (a)mwa (lu).

263.  1st line, add (mwa ǫṅwu, person dead).

264.  To na, upon, add in, at, to, from.
Under (a)na *go*, go (home), for onaka nakǫ read
ǫnakǫ anakǫ; onakinakǫ read ǫnak' inakǫ.

265.  2nd line, for mwade read mwado.
For (a)nakulu, go back to old husband, read (a)nak-
wulu.
For (a)nakulu, go to visit, read (a)nakwulu.
For (a)napaga read (a)napųga.
2nd line from end, add snatch away.

266.  1st line, add be mad.
6th line from top, for ǫlo read ǫlų.
For nbęlęju, sherd, read (mbelęju), sherd.

267.  Indented under ṅčę̈zǫ̈' insert di ṅčę̈zǫ̈, forgettable.

269.  1st line, for ṅdęli read ṅdęlè.
3rd line for ndendo read ndendų.
To ndi, *forms noun with verb*, add *also plural of
onye*.

270.  For ndǫzo, full moon, read ndǫzu.
For ndu, larvæ found on tombo tree, read ndu, larva
of tombo fly.

271.  For (e)ne unene l' ainya read (e)nę' unęnęl'
      ainya.
      For (e)nečem *lu* nče read (e)neče *lu* nče.
      To (e)nefega, pass, add look over.
272.  (e)neta (mętu aka), for took read look.
      For (i)ni (A), cry, read (a)nĭ.
      To (a)nia *lu,* neglect, add cry as child.
      (e)nifue, for loose read lose.
      To (e)niri, go, go away, start, add break off.
      Delete eniri (O), stand up.
      For nĵak' obi read nĵa k'obi.
273.  After nĵĭ' (A), enmity, insert onye nĵi', enemy.
      3rd line from end, for being eaten as food, read eating
      food.
274.  To ñloyà, making up mind, add changing mind.
      For ñlotà, remembering, read (di) ñlotà.
275.  To nni (O), food, add pounded yam.
      To nnono mili, etc., add water bird.
276.  Under (a)nǫ, be, for anǫm umwa read anǫmu
      mwa.
      Under (a)nǫ, live, for nazulike read naizulike.
      Under (a)nǫ *gu,* stay, for aĵamanǫ read agam
      anǫ.
277.  2nd line, for agamanatowa read agam anot' owa.
      For (e)nočibe read (a)nǫčibe.
      To (a)nǫdu *lu* (ǫdo), sit, add stay long.
      To (a)nǫyalie, etc., add turn round.
278.  3rd line for (a)nokwasi read (a)nǫkwasi.
      For n'oso, apart, read n'osǫ́.
      nrai (O), partition, read nrainye.
279.  1st line, add service, bondage.
      2nd line, for åwkålům read kålům.
      To nruru ǫku, heat, hot, add unhealthy.
      For nseliazu, bustard, read bustard (?) heron (?).
280.  nsuęñwe, squirrel, for *Euxerus erythropus* read
      *Protoxerus stangeri ebori-vorus.*
281.  For ñtì ainya read ñtì ainya.

To ntite, rotten part of cloth, tree, add for rubbing floor.

Delete, ntite, rubbing house.

To ńtitú, knocking down, add blow of hammer.

To ńto, mortal disease, etc., add ? ptomaine poisoning.

For nṭobẹ (O), putting medicine in gate, read nṭụbẹ, and add crossing fingers.

282.  For ńtotà, coming out of ambush, read ńtŏtà.

For ńṭoṭà, picking up, read ńṭŏṭà.

ńtù ẹbi (A.O), nail, delete (A) ẹbì, ebinta.

283.  To (e)nú'e, buy palm wine, add or drink.

To (e)nulu óḳu, etc., hear cause of palaver.

284.  Under nya, him, her, for forọ read fụrọ.

For (ai) nya alo, be heavy, read nyị alo.

8th line from end, for (active) read (*active*).

Indented under (ai)nyaka *lu*, for out read only.

To (ai)nyi, be satiated, add weighty.

285.  To (ai)nyi, pass, add surpass.

4th line from end, for ọinyokudolum read ọinyokudolu.

3rd line from end, for nyukudo read nyukwudo.

Last line, add let me go and urinate.

286.  To ńzẹ̀ (A), breathing in, add asking.

287.  To ṅzúzu, hiding, add secret.

For ng'abug'ẹ read ṅgabugẹ.

For ṅgà̀dà read ńgạdà.

288.  ngederi (A), since this morning, a long time, delete since this morning.

For ngi, you read ngị, thou.

289.  For ṅgwạligọdọ read ṅgwọligọdọ.

For ṅgwe onọmuzọ read ṅgwe ụnọmụzọ, and add seat outside.

Under ñgwọ̀, *Raphia vinifera*, for I have a tombo tree read I have a big tombo tree.

291.  For nkɓ ọkọ (A), fish fence read nkɓọkọ, and insert whole before ṅkɓokọ (A), heap.

To ṅkɓọ, wedge, add hook.

292.  For ńkɓǫpo, jump read ńkɓǫpo.
      For ǹkɓù anthill read ǹkɓú.
      For nkɓumkɓu read ǹkɓuǹkɓu.

293.  For nkętịgwe, meteor, read nkętịgwe (or nkịtịgwe),
      meteor, ńko, sharp (fig.), delete (fig.), and for ńko
      read (di)ńko.
      For nkoifia read ǹkoifia (or ǹkoipia).
      Delete last line.

294.  Under ǹkṕǫ́' (O), calabash, for éje read éjì.

296.  nkụja (A), jump (with fear), delete (A).
      To nkukoba (A), knot, add overhand knot.
      nkunili (mili), (ume) delete mili; add nkunili
      mili drawing in water.
      For ǹkwádobe (A), beginning, read ǹkwádębe.

297.  To nkwò (O), plucking, add (fowl).
      To ǹkwǫ́ (A), kite, add (bird).
      For nkwukwoba read ǹkwụkwụba.
      4th line from end, add borrow iyi.

298.  For ǹpača, careful, read ǹkpača.
      For ǹpakęlečǫ read ǹkpakęlečǫ, and add two balls
      on string as plaything.
      For ǹpǫ́kǫ read ǹkpǫ́kǫ.
      For ǹpokpoala read ǹkṕokṕoala.
      For ǹpok'wa read ǹkṕokwa.
      5th line from end read ǹwǎbǫ̈.
      3rd line from end, delete unmarriageable.

299.  For ǹwagęlęli, small line, read ǹwagęlęle.
      To nwaiyǫ, slow, add quiet.

300.  1st line, add customers.
      2nd line from top, for (e)ǹwe read (e)ǹwö̀.
      To (e)ǹwęlu *gu* di, etc., add be married.
      To (e)ǹwo *lu*, be ill, add (change).
      Under (e)ǹwo *lu*, for ąró ǫǹwuǹwu; naǹwum read
      ąrụ ǫǹwuǹwu naǹwum.

301.  To (e)ǹwu ǫ́kò (A), add burn.
      For (a)nwu totaǹgwęle read (a)ǹwụ tataǹgwęle.
      Delete (a)ǹwude, catch.

To (a)ṅwufue aṅwufue, etc., add die away.

302. Under obá̧, person with many children, for ŏmŏt̯ålŏ
ŏmŏ nŏbȁ' read ŏmṷt̯ålŏ ṵmṵ nŏbȁ.
obȁ̧' (A), menstrual blood, delete (A).
For obã̈, calabash read obwã̈.
To obe (O), disease, etc., add or prominent vein in new
born.

303. 2nd line from top, for ṁbe'ku read ṁbȩku.
For obíntò read obínlò.

304. For o̧bò, or, read o̧bṵ.
2nd line from top, for o̧bŏ read o̧bṷ.
óbo (A), spear, etc. delete (A) and add (broad and
long).
For obó ȩkwȩ read obwó ȩkwȩ.
For o̧bòlona, if, read ó̧bõ̧lṵna, if.
obŏbȁ' (O), being open, etc., for (in market) read (of
market).

305. For o̧bó̧gò (O), duck, read o̧bó̧gṵ.
For óbòna (A), spear, read ób̧(w)õna.

306. To o̧bṵbṵ (O), person who has eaten too much, add
overgrown.

307. Delete obã̈lu (ono̧).
3rd line from end, for o̧bwádo, read o̧bwádṵ.

308. To obwano̧koko, crane (white), add ?egret.
obwó̧ (O), cause, for cause read canoe.
2nd line from end, for ŏbŏ read ŏbwŏ.
Last line, for cause read canoe.

309. For o̧čá, white, read o̧čá (or o̧iča), white.
For oči̧ča', cockroach, read oči̧ča' (or ṵčiča), cock-
roach.
For očĭči, darkness, read očĭči (or ṵčĭči), darkness.

310. For odači, dead man, read odači dalo, dead man.
To odefinewu (O), knot, add running knot to
hold.
odide (A), wet (salt) delete (salt).

311. Under odinka (A), for, for *lu* read lu, and for lin
yak read tiny' ak'.

312.  For odǫgodǫ read odǫyodǫ.
313.  For odu afia read odu oifia.
      odudu enyi, fly (tsetse) for tsetse, read mangrove
      fly.
314.  For ofîbo read ofîbo.
      Under ǫ́fǒ, new, for ǫ́fǒ ǫfǒ read ǫ́fụ̀ ǫfǒ.
      For ŏfo, sight, read ŏfụ.
315.  Under ofu aka, same, for madụ read mwadụ.
      For ogǎ', girls' game, read ŏga' (or ŏgà), girls'
      game.
316.  ǫgálẹ̀ (O), knife, small, delete (O).
      For ǫgẹ̀nǎzò (O), fish bone, spine, read ǫgẹ̀nǎzụ̀, and
      delete spine.
317.  2nd line, delete?
318.  ǫ̌gùgù (O), innumerable, for innumerable read
      numerable, to be counted.
      To ŏgugu, raphia leaf, add oil palm branch.
319.  For ógwǫ', debt, read ụ́gwǫ' and insert onye ụ́gwǫ',
      debtor.
      For ǫ́gwò, medicine, read ǫ́gwụ, and under ǫ́gwụ, read
      ògwụ̌ ògwụ̌.
320.  For oḥǔḥù read oḥǔḥù.
      For ǫinyálà, madman, read (onye ala) ǫinyálà.
322.  To ojuku, tree, add oil palm with white nuts.
324.  okꞵó, game (catching of ankle) for of read by.
      For ókꞵǫ, red yam species read red yams grated.
      To okꞵokꞵa, divining string, add (palm nuts).
325.  To ǫ̀kꞵókꞵo, work in common, add help in palaver.
      For òkꞵokꞵo, bone, read ǫ̀kꞵokꞵo.
      For okꞵŏkolo, bachelor, read okꞵŏkolo  (or
      okokꞵolo), bachelor.
      For ǫkbolalaka ṅwạinye  read  ǫkbolalaka
      ṅwạinye.
326.  2nd line from top, for ókwo read úkwụ.
      For okꞵŏrò (O), woman, read okꞵŏrǫ̀ (or okporo)
      (O), woman.
      For ǫkbotǫlǫkꞵu read ǫkꞵụtǫlǫkꞵu.

328. Indented under o̩kı̀lı̀ (O), plague, for (plague take
you) read (plague kill you).
Indented under ó̩ko', fire, for ò̩kò̩ ońyé ò̩ké read
o̩kò̩ ońyé o̩kò̩, and for on fire read on the fire.

329. Last line, delete (O).

330. For o̩ko̩l'ololo read o̩ko̩l'u̩tu̩lu̩.
okoto (O), corner, delete (O).

331. oku̩ku̩ńwa (O), for hip read lisp.

333. To olia (O), cry of baby, add sickness.

334. 2nd line from top, add (*Euxerus erythropus*).
5th line from top, for under read upper.
For ólilò̩', thinking, read ólilò̩.
For ő̩lo̩', mud, read ő̩lo̩' (or ólo'), mud.
For olokwo (O), thigh (o̩lookwo), read o̩lo̩kwu̩
(O), thigh (o̩lou̩kwu̩).

335. For òmi̩me (A), bearing, read òmi̩mì.

336. For o̩momo, bearing (children), read o̩mu̩mu̩.
To omu̩čam (O), gun, add cap.

337. For ŏ̩nà ókù (O), ring (foot), read ŏ̩na ú̩kwu̩.
óni (A), yam stick, delete (A) and add (large).
To ono̩ńkpo̩wa, etc., add bachelor's house.
onu ofifie, torticoltis, for torticoltis read torticollis.
For ó̩nu o̩fife, slip of tongue, read o̩nu̩ o̩fifie.
For onú údùdà, person with goitre, read onu údùdu.
For onu údúdà, pot with neck, read o̩nu údúdù,
pot with long neck.

339. 2nd line from top, add vexation.

341. To ó̩nyínyé, giving, add gift.
To ó̩ńo, rejoicing, add Schadenfreude.

342. 1st line, add craftsman.

343. For ò̩ro̩lwíte, taking pot from fire, read ò̩ro̩fuíte.
2nd line from end, for óru ò̩sà read oru o̩sà.

344. For osá' (A), village that is dying out, read (nd') osá.
2nd line from end, add answer.

345. osisiǎdogo (O) read top of tree cut down and coming
into leaf.
To ő̩só', bat (big), add *Eidolon helvum*

346.  For otako aka (A), half of chest, read back of upper
      arm.
      To ọte (O), hunter's path, add lair.
      For oté nme read oté mme.
347.  Last line, add cane.
348.  Indented under ọ̃tọ́tọ́ (O), many, insert ọtọtọ ẹgo,
      much money.
349.  To ovuvu, big, add overgrown.
      ọwalámb̃wo (A), etc., for panel read frame.
      To owẽle, bush near back of house, add woman's
      latrine.
351.  To ọzãla (O), etc., add prairie.
      To ŏzì (O), drum (big), add (abia).
      To ọ̀zɪ̃za, swelling on foot or hand, add bruise.
      After ọzízọ̀, saving, curing, insert onye ọzízọ̀
      helper.
352.  1st line, before house insert (man's).
      For òzò, noise, read ụ̀zụ̀.
      For òzọ̃, early, read ụzọ̃.
      For ózọ ide read ụzọ ide, and add furrow.
      For ọzọ̃ potam read ọzọ̃potam.
      For ozũzò, tying knot, read ozũzụ.
353.  For (a)painiyite read (a)painyite.
      To (a)patue, etc., add carry down.
      For (á)pẹ̀ (A), give, read (á)pẹ̃.
      To (a)pia, press, add squeeze.
      To (a)pia apiã, "be sleepy" (of fruit), add empty.
      To (a)pia apɪ̃a, spoil (seed), add be smashed.
      To arụ (a)pia (A), be sickly, add tired.
354.  2nd line from top, add be able.
      To (a)pụa iče, be different, add go alone.
      To (a)puzie, move a little, add go out.
355.  To (a)ra amu, etc., add sound.
      To (a)ra ịgwa (O), etc., add march.
      For (a)ru *lu* kà read (a)ra *lu* kà.
      To (a)ra mili, etc., add draw water.
      Last line, add abandon.

356. Under (a)rapu *go*, leave off, read rapu if' ịẹkọ.
     For (e)rẹk'po *lu* read (e)rẹkpo *lu*.
357. 1st line, for (a)ri *li* read (a)ri (ari) *li*.
     Under (e)rọ (O), hang, for *gu* read gu.
     To (a)rọ squeeze, add bruise, mash.
358. (e)ropu *lu*, pull out, after (e)ropu insert (eropu).
     (a)rọta *lu*, pick good one, read pick (good) one.
     (a)rụ ọnu, fix price (two owners), read (of owner).
     For (e)rubuata *lu* read (e)rubwata *lu*.
359. 5th line from top, add make person wet.
     To (e)rulu erulu, add sit with head on hands.
     To (e)rulu nrulu, add bend head.
     To (e)rusisie (O), etc., add scatter.
     For (a)rᵚorᵚoa, toy (?), read arᵚorᵚoa.
360. (a)sainye, teach medicine, read teach (medicine);
     open and show.
     2nd line from end, add stir food.
361. 4th line from top, add draw back.
     Indented under (e)selie, stretch, read ume (e)sẹpu.
     For (a)seta *lu*, lie, read (e)seta *lu*, esẹtam.
362. Under (e)si, tread, to ọkuko nẹsi ẹsi, add the cock
     treads the fowl.
     For (e)si anádi, look, read (e)si àná di.
     2nd line from end, for (e)sie, read (a)sie.
363. 5th line from top, add dye.
     6th line from top, add cook together.
     Under sọ, only, alone, for ịjemsọm read ẹjemsọm.
     4th line from end, add make stupid.
     2nd line from end, add be long.
364. (e)su *lu* obundu, for fire, cannon, read fire cannon.
365. 1st line, add jabber.
     To (e)sue *lu*, dip, add (only eatable).
     To (e)susulu, give some one a taste of, add kiss.
366. To (a)ta bulibuli, be talkative, add be vexed.
     For (a)ta nkkele ẹze, read (a)ta nkekele ẹze.
     To (a)ta' *lu* ntamu, whisper, add grumble.
     To (a)ta' ọji (A), be bribed, add eat kola.

To (a)tacie *li*, persevere, add dry off.

To (a)tådò, be patient, add bite.

To (a)tagide, stick to, add keep chewing.

367.  1st line, for (a)tăkunye read (a)tăkwunye.

To tatangwęle, etc., add " foot asleep."

368.  To tępu tępu, plump, add soft.

For (e)ti, shout, read (e)tie, and for oti (e)ti, have fever, read oti (e)tie.

To (e)tibe, blow (*intrans*), add hit and break.

To (e)tie *lu* k'ǫnwa, shine, add (like moon).

For (e)tie ǫka n'ǫko, read (e)tie ǫko n'ǫko.

369.  For (e)tiwa *lu*, break (pot), read (e)tiwa (ętiwa) *lu*.

For (e)tì *lu*, praise, read (e)tö *lu*.

370.  1st line add (single large drops) ; drip (water, honey).

For (a)to timęte, slacken, be loose, read (a)tǫ tunęte.

For (a)tǫ (nte), spread, read (a)tö (ute).

To (a)toa dig, add (yams).

under (a)toa, wet, for ętol' read atol', and for wet read wets.

371.  (a)toa ntò, tie, for tie read lie.

To (a)toba *lu* ainya, look for, add (you).

For atǫbę *lu* ǫgu read (a)tǫbę *lu* ǫgu.

2nd line from end, add lie still.

372.  To (a)toka, cut (very small branches) add with stone.

To (a)to *lu* *gu* unǫ, build, add put on mats.

under (e)tote (O), order, for dniweniye read dinweniye.

373.  For (na)tu *lu* ezu, read (na)tu *lu* egu.

last line, add find fault.

374.  3rd line from top, for (a)tufu, read (e)tufu.

For (a)tyiapu *lu*, read (a)tyrapu *lu*.

For (a)tukp̣o mili, throw on body with hand, read (e)tukp̣o.

For (a)tulukǫba read (a)tutukǫba.

375.  For ubú (O), net, etc., read ybwų́.

For úbwŏdò (O), companion, read úbwŏlò.

376.  To ùdù, pot, used by girls for song, add water pot.

377.   To ùke', hindrance, trouble, add ill-luck.
       To ukệle, cleverness, add lively.
378.   8th line from top, delete hole, in tree.
379.   To úmệ' (A), power, add loins.
380.   5th line from top, delete (A).
       To ùmwapià, twisting add ệkwệli string.
       umwaro, boy (small), for boy read boys.
       Delete 4th line from end.
381.   ute ajịbi (O) utenká (A) for (igara) read
           (Igara).
       uvệle (O), bolt, read (cross bow).
       4th line from end delete (A).
382.   To ụzọ read add way, manner, time.
       Insert v seems to be unvoiced in the following words.
383.   To (e)yu ụzọ, go first, add (A).
       For (a)wa, cut, break (kola), read (a)wả' (or wå), cut
           break (kola).
384.   Under (a)waba (A), be open, for anarano read
           amarano.
       For wanya (A), mwọ, read wanya (A), more.
       For (e)wari, be broken, read (e)ware.
       For (e)wệce li, take first, read (e)wèce li.
       For (e)weda ọṅwe, read (e) weda oṅwě.
       For (e)wedu, be angry, read (e)wedo.
385.   To (e)wệnie aka, hold up hand, add abandon.
       To (e)wệruka lu, separate, add take out of the way.
       To (a)woba, jump, add jump in ; for alolo read
           atolo, and for amara read amwara.
386.   Nor (a)wukọ read (e)wukọ, and add cook together.
       To (a)wunye, pour into pot, add put yams in pot.
387.   1st line, add be cooked.
388.   5th line from top for sweep, read support.
       For (a)začiệ, swell, read (a)zači.
       To (e)zedo lu, defend, protect, add lean something
           against.
       Last line for (a)zi read (e)zi'.
389.   For (e)zo kola, read (e)zo, transplant (kola).

390.   5th line from top, add grumble.

For (e)zu, trade, read (a)zụ.

For (e)zu afia, trade, read (a)zụ afia.

(ẹ)zǔbě (O), learn, for learn read thieve.

To (a)zuƀuě, swindle, add kill.

3rd line from end add to 2.0 p.m.